To Suzanne,

Eric

D1736873

i

Who Murdered FDR?

Copyright 2016 by Stephen B. Ubaney

Additional copies may be ordered at:
www.whomurderedbooks.com
www.facebook.com/Who-Murdered-FDR

ISBN: 978-0-9882829-3-3 (Softcover)
ISBN: 978-0-9882829-5-7 (eBook)
ASIN: B01MSCY6RL (Audiobook)

Dedication

To the most wonderful parents anyone could ask for. You give so much and ask so little.

Author's Note

I was a good student. I completed three degrees in three years, was inducted into national and international honor societies, and graduated in the top 1% of my class at the University at Buffalo. I read all the right books, asked all the right questions and took all the right notes.

I learned a great deal from my teachers and professors, but I always knew that schools only educated people; they couldn't teach them how to think. I realized that even the most decorated of students were doing little more than repeating what we had been told and reciting sentences from books, written by God-knows-who, that all said the same basic thing.

It wasn't until years later that I figured out that those textbooks were selected that way for a reason. The textbooks were selected by the same people who were teaching us not think on our own. Are we breeding a society of mental sheep? Doesn't sheep rhyme with sleep?!

As the years went by I developed something that I called the "five times rule". When there was something that I couldn't get to the bottom of, I asked myself why. Each time I came to an answer, I asked why again, and I kept doing it until I got to the root of the issue. I am certainly no genius, but I was able to solve more than a few of life's little puzzles this way.

In the years that followed I developed a great interest in revisiting the text books that we were forced to read in many of those torturous classrooms.

History and World War II were subjects that especially interested me, so I put the *five times rule* to work on my favorite events within those subjects. This book is the result of four years of exercising the *five times rule* on a subject that I never believed happened the way that they said.

I put the *five times rule* to work on one question that has dogged me for years. How could President Roosevelt, Adolph Hitler, and Benito Mussolini all end up dead in a little over two weeks? When I unpacked that question, other questions began to surround me.

Why was Stalin so paranoid about everyone around him? How did President Roosevelt conveniently die just as Allied troops were reaching Hitler's bunker? Why wasn't Roosevelt autopsied or embalmed? Why, in 1957, did Eleanor Roosevelt hire a private investigator to reopen the case of her husband's death? What was she looking for?

This book consists of three years of solid mental digging as I read, researched, and uncovered lost treasures in the national archives that I used to answer my questions. What I have discovered at the end of my exhaustive investigation flies in the face of the history textbooks that we were commanded to believe.

Over time I have grown to hate the *five times rule*, as it is more of a curse than a blessing. I am genuinely sorry for having uncovered some of the things I did, and this is the vanguard of those times. Those living under the misconception that this book was just written to make a quick buck have obviously never written a book.

I can't begin to tell you the painstaking hours that have gone into the research, writing, phone calling, and the gathering of the necessary facts and permissions. There is no way I could ever be paid enough for this book to be a profitable venture, so I will take my pension in the knowledge that the truth will finally be told.

Introduction

This book is presented solely for entertainment purposes. It is a creative nonfiction book that weaves a hypothesis based on years of researched facts. Some of these facts have existed in other authors' works for decades and have been presented within this manuscript to assist the author and reader, with the development of the storyline.

In order to get as close to the truth as humanly possible, the material selected for presentation dealt only in first hand experiences and were of the best "source direct" content available.

While the best efforts have been used in preparing this book, and the author has quoted several official and credible sources, the content is a narrative of those gathered facts. The author is not a professional law enforcement agent or criminal investigator.

This book was written without ghost writers, malice or ulterior motives. The author's sole intention is to solve the long standing mystery surrounding President Roosevelt's death and not to discredit or defame any character in the manuscript's factual hypothesis.

The opinion(s) expressed in this book may not be the personal opinion(s) of the author. It is merely a gathering of researched fact based on the information available.

The literary journalism within this book has finally assembled a believable and final event out of the scrambled and conflicting reports which have been repeatedly warped in the public consciousness for years.

Those who read this book the first time will do so to learn about Franklin Roosevelt's murder. Those who read this book the second time will do so to try and wrap their minds around how deeply the powers behind the murder went. Those who read this book a third time will never look at the hierarchical powers in this world the same way again.

Those who are thanked

Wm. E. Weller Esq

J. Richard Milazzo Esq

Brandon Borden

Those who are acknowledged

David Vona, MD

Jim Ostrowski, Esq

Debora Becerra, Esq

Mark Lane, Esq

Those who inspired

Gerard Crinnin, PhD

Mark Lane, Esq

Richard Hugo

Robert Nasca

Cyril H. Wecht, M.D., J.D.

From the author of the eye-opening book -
Who Murdered Elvis?

1
The Chronicle

"I do not believe in Communism any more than you do but there is nothing wrong with the Communists in this country; several of the best friends I have got are Communists."

- Franklin Delano Roosevelt -

History is a funny thing. It belongs largely to those in academia who approve the textbooks and the core curriculum that we learn from. But outside of the watered down version of what we have all been taught exists a vast array of truth that we must all absorb if we desire to digest the facts.

This has never been more evident than in the circumstances surrounding Franklin Roosevelt's rise to political power, presidency, and inevitable murder. The first two chapters of this book will recap and quantify the history that we have already been told, but I must apologize in advance: it has a political slant.

There is nothing that I hate more than politics or the political arguments that are promoted by the 24-hour media that continuously tell you how to think and feel, but I had to go that route for several pages to reveal the murder suspects as the book progresses. There is a method to my madness, there always is, so understand why I am taking you there. Political leanings aside, my only intention is to set the stage for the murder.

This will be shocking, but the other side of history is quick to reveal that President Roosevelt was indeed a Communist. FDR loved the Communist ideology, but these facts have been covered up by the news media and the unions in academia, and I don't expect that to change anytime soon.

While labeling FDR as a Communist in today's world may seem shocking, in the 1930's and 1940's it was commonplace. That era knew nothing about the Cold War, Evil Empires, nuclear weapons or the Communist plan to take the countries of the world over one at a time. Communism was in its infancy, and many people were misled by its propaganda. Americans during the early 1900's were tempted to cast asunder the traditional American faith in Capitalism in the exploration of a better system, and many of them did.

After all, the entire American system of government on the whole was an experiment upon its inception. At that time every government in the world was established by the denial of their citizens' rights, America was formed by affirming its citizen rights. Even this didn't satisfy the ruling class from fooling our citizens into looking for something better.

Many Americans looked to Communism as a new system of government that was better than our Capitalist society. They viewed it as a system of government without risk, without need, and without the fear of strife. It didn't make them bad people; they were just curious and misled. This is the era that Franklin Roosevelt was born into, and that groomed his political acumen.

The year was 1912 and America was a very different place than what we are used to. Einstein's theory of relativity was a new and unproven idea. Telephone calls, motion pictures, the Army tank, the pop-up toaster and the zipper were all new innovations. The Panama Canal, New York's Grand Central Terminal and Boston's Fenway Park were all newly opened. It was a time before Babe Ruth, crossword puzzles, canned beer, or even iced tea.

The average American worker made between $150 and $450 per year; 20% of American adults were illiterate with only 7% of the nation's population having graduated from high school. People were largely uneducated and constitutionally naïve.

Their access to what was really going on in their government was restricted to newspapers and the people who controlled them. This was the same year that President Woodrow Wilson appointed FDR to assistant secretary of the Navy.

With a largely ignorant and disconnected American population the stage was perfectly set for the introduction of Communist ideas, and Woodrow Wilson was the perfect US Presidential Candidate to introduce them.

President Wilson was an interesting fellow. Wilson's father was a slave-owning Confederate who moved his family south during the Civil War. His father eventually taught college and convinced the sickly Woodrow to do the same. Woodrow, realizing that he couldn't do physical labor, devoted his life to his studies.

He attended Davidson College, Princeton and later the University of Virginia Law School. Accompanying his law studies were the pursuits of political philosophy and history. Wilson was admitted to the Georgia bar association and briefly practiced law, but soon discovered that he hated the United States Constitution and the daily application of its practices. He quickly abandoned his law practice and obtained his PhD at John's Hopkins University.

He became a professor and began lecturing at Cornell University and Bryn Mawr College. After a short time the restless Wilson broke his employment contracts with Bryn Mawr and Wesleyan University. With the aid of his many friends in academia he was elected to the board at Princeton and was eventually promoted to President of the University in June 1902.

During his time at Princeton he lectured and openly expressed his disdain for the United States Constitution. He opposed the Constitution's three separate branches of government, favoring the Parliamentary system where the executive and legislative branches are interconnected and the President could make and control laws as he saw fit. He was preaching a platform where one leader would have total control of the United States government.

In an effort to try to convince the populace that his ideas of governing were superior, he published three works that Franklin Roosevelt read and studied with great enthusiasm. They were the *Congressional Government, The State,* and the *Constitutional Government of the United States*.

The summary of these writings revealed Woodrow Wilson's anti-American platform as he ridiculed America's system of checks and balances, writing that the presidency *"will be as big as and as influential as the man who occupies it"*.

Wilson's growing reputation through his published works and his ability to communicate his ideas led Democrats to consider him as a viable Presidential candidate. Further posturing himself in the political arena he was elected to the Governorship of New Jersey in 1910.

While in office he met and befriended Edward Mandell House. House, or "Colonel" House as he was called, was a powerful American diplomat and politician. He soon became Wilson's presidential advisor, and would go on to head Wilson's Presidential campaign. With the Republican vote divided between two candidates Wilson won the 1912 Presidential election with forty-two percent of the vote.

Once elected, the grateful Woodrow Wilson granted Colonel House great involvement in his new administration. House was a Marxist, and a very dangerous political manipulator. At the time, the American people had no idea that Colonel House had recently authored a novel that mapped out the transformation of the United States to a Communist State. In a truly cowardly act, House's Communist writings were published under a pen name whose identity took decades to unravel.

The two men became so inseparable that it was rumored, although incorrectly, that they were a homosexual couple and that they were in love. Wilson would go on to delegate numerous executive decisions to his politically likeminded soul-mate, who had influence over everything and was held accountable for nothing.

In regard to Colonel House, Wilson would eventually claim that *"Mr. House is my second personality. He is my independent self. His thoughts and mine are one."* With Wilson's political mind perfectly synced to a Marxist, the damage that would be done to dissolve America's freedoms and its Democracy at the urging of Colonel House would be devastating, and the ever-curious Roosevelt closely monitored every move that they made.

Within no time the ten steps (or ten planks) that are outlined in the Communist Manifesto for transforming a free society to a communist society were slowly enacted by the Wilson-House administration. The first plank was the establishment of a graduated income tax to penalize those working the hardest and to prevent them from bettering themselves.

Wealth is not part of the Marxist plan, so earners must be punished. The second plank of the Communist Manifesto was the abolition of all rights of inheritance. This basically means that an inheritance tax puts all money that would be passed down to another person in jeopardy. Karl Marx believed that the abolishment of inheritance would be part of a natural progression toward the collectivist state of Communism.

He believed that that the private ownership of land and the "means of production" should be discontinued by force. With this plank, which gave the government control over the means of production, there would no longer be privately held wealth to pass down.

The third and final plank was accomplished by bullying Congress into passing a law to seize gold and other hard currency from banks and to centralize the monetary system. The system was then put under the control of a private monopoly of unelected elitists.

This was known to you and me as the creation of the Federal Reserve. Running true-to-form, Colonel House and Woodrow Wilson were slowly seizing wealth from the people and turning it over to the government for their use and control.

Mercifully for the United States of America, two gigantic diversions presented themselves requiring President Wilson's full attention. These took his mind away from fulfilling the last seven planks in the Communist Manifesto. Wilson's wife died of kidney failure, and he would go on to suffer a debilitating stroke.

His stroke was so severe that his second wife, Edith, was actually running the country. With the help of their many friends in government she was able to fool Wilson's cabinet, the press corps, and Congress, into concealing the severity of his affliction.

This was done by enlisting the help of Rear Admiral Cary Grayson. Grayson was a surgeon in the United States Navy who was summoned by Wilson's wife to examine the President. He would eventually go on to serve as Wilson's personal aide as well as chairman of the American Red Cross.

There is an interesting quote in the book *FDR's Deadly Secret* that explains how that happened. "Grayson conspired with Wilson's second wife, Edith (whom he'd first introduced to the president), to deceive the cabinet, Congress, and the American people about the perilous state of his health. Wilson was largely kept hidden from public view, including visitors from Capitol Hill and even the president's own aides."

President Wilson, at the urging of Colonel House, appointed Franklin Roosevelt to Assistant Secretary of the Navy. Teddy Roosevelt had served as President from 1901 to 1909. After his death in 1919, Teddy Roosevelt's eight-year Presidency had taken on near mythical proportions, and the last name of Roosevelt held great power in the country at that time.

There, under this role, FDR could learn rapidly from his two communist masters. The complete conversion of this country into the desired Marxist state would have to wait until Franklin Delano Roosevelt took office two decades later.

In reality, Franklin was studying the inner-workings of the Wilson-House policies far more than he ever studied in college and not everyone was happy about it. Many people viewed FDR as a political "flip-flopper."

FDR's father, James Roosevelt, was a Democrat, and his presidential cousin, Theodore Roosevelt, was a Republican. This proved to be an issue when James met his bride-to-be, Sara Delano. Sara's father, Warren Delano, disliked Theodore for his political affiliation and told James that "not every Democrat he'd met was a horse thief, but every horse thief he'd met was a Democrat." FDR appeared to be insulting the former President as well as many of his cousins.

The problem for young Franklin was that he was completely out of touch with common people. Not only did he not know how to solve their problems, but he couldn't identify with their problems. Horses, carriages, boats, guns, candy, fishing poles and even colleges were his for the asking and he received them all with little effort.

Attending both Harvard University and Columbia Law School while producing sub-par grades, his family's money pushed him forward while his presidential cousin, who was in office at that time, was clearing his way to stardom.

FDR wanted for nothing, and no human being benefited more from the lucky sperm club than he did. He was a Roosevelt, and he was born to be king. Since Teddy Roosevelt was in office during Franklin's college years it should surprise no one that upon Franklin's graduation he was elected to the New York State Senate.

There would be no other way that a heavily Republican area would elect a Democrat, except for the last name of Roosevelt. It was after this term, and after heavily following the Wilson-House agenda, that he was appointed Assistant Secretary of the Navy. This made him the youngest person in US history to hold the position. Again, it would be no coincidence that his famous cousin and US President, Teddy Roosevelt, had previously held the same record and the same office.

Amazingly, FDR had turned down other governmental appointments to accept that position. He had watched Cousin Teddy's road to the White House and had set out to hit the same stops along the way.

Franklin Roosevelt's motivation to capture the White House also led to him marrying his own cousin, Eleanor, who was also a cousin of President Teddy Roosevelt. Eleanor was born a Roosevelt, married a Roosevelt and died a Roosevelt.

It became clear to everyone watching this unfold that FDR was capable of magnificent insincerity. Even the park rangers who give the guided tours of the Roosevelt Mansion in Hyde Park, NY, seriously question the motivation of the marriage.

To underscore the political convenience of this marriage, the person who gave Eleanor away at her wedding was none of than the President of the United States of America, and her uncle, Teddy Roosevelt.

To further boggle the mind, immediately after the wedding ceremony Teddy congratulated his fifth cousin Franklin telling him "that-a-boy for keeping the name in the family." Following the attention that Theodore Roosevelt's death had received, and the wave of national sentiment for their fallen hero, the Roosevelt name couldn't have been more popular.

In 1920 the benefactor of this sentimentality would be the thirty-eight-year-old Franklin as he received the Vice-Presidential nod from Governor Jim Cox of Ohio. This was bittersweet for Franklin. He enjoyed the national notoriety, but the political party in power after a war rarely stays in power and Cox's resulting loss started Roosevelt's life on a downward spiral.

Call it cruel fate, a long overdue comeuppance, or just simply bad luck, but shortly after receiving so much attention and notoriety FDR became paralyzed from the neck down. It took almost three weeks for the doctors to diagnose the condition as Polio (or Infantile Paralysis, as it was known at the time).

During the weeks that it took for the doctors to establish their diagnosis, a grievous error was made. By not putting him in an iron lung to safeguard his breathing Franklin nearly died. The final diagnosis was actually good news for FDR, as with polio there is always a chance that the afflicted limbs can be rejuvenated through hard work.

After first getting movement in his fingers, and then after weeks of hard work in his arms, he had a bar installed over his bed so he could do pull-ups to attempt to strengthen the rest of his body. Eventually he was able to regain movement all the way down to his hips but that's where his progress ended. Searching for answers to revive his limbs he found Warm Springs, Georgia. There he was able to stand on his own and exercise his feeble legs in the hot mineral waters.

At Hyde Park he developed his own exercise regimen. Parallel bars were put in the yard, and he forced himself to walk the quarter mile from the mansion to Route 9 with ten-pound steel braces under his pants locking his hips, knees and ankles in place.

In reality, what he did was drag himself the entire way to his destination and back again with crutches under his arms. His motivation was not just to walk again but to reenter political life. At that time it was believed that if you had a physical disability you must have a mental disability as well.

His motivation was twofold. In trying to regain the use of his lower extremities he had to struggle at something for the first time in his life. He genuinely began to care about the suffering of those sick and less fortunate.

It was this disability that helped the future President Roosevelt to connect with common people and their struggles in a way that no President before him had. This life altering event convinced Roosevelt that the federal government should become the caretaker of its less fortunate citizens in a *cradle-to-grave* capacity.

This belief usurped the traditional role of the Christian church which had established most of the nation's hospitals, clinics and charitable organizations. In 1928, Franklin had taken his new message of caring for the sick and less fortunate back into the political world, winning him the Governorship of the State of New York.

Running in his own backyard ensured his victory regardless of his physical condition, keeping him in the public eye and fulfilling his need for status and power. In New York his ability to endure physical trials won the respect of many of the voters, but he would soon go to great lengths to conceal his disability, as his true ambition was, and always been, to own the White House.

Soon, specially fitted leg and back braces were crafted out of heavy steel, allowing him to stand erect for extended periods of time in the public eye. They gave Roosevelt the illusion of fitness while his legs were in the most atrophied of conditions.

He also devised an ingenious method of taking short steps with a cane in one hand while calling upon the arm of a personal aide with the other. In politics, unlike many other forms of life, the illusion of substance is far different than the reality of it, and Franklin Roosevelt was the master of illusion.

The Democrats, as much then as today, had the full cooperation of the press, as, in the span of eighteen months, several planted newspaper articles were printed portraying Roosevelt as making a full recovery from his polio affliction.

They attempted to rebuild Roosevelt's credibility and fool the American people in the process. One report even went so far as to say that he had "discarded the crutches" entirely. The book *FDR's Deadly Secret* quoted the following:

> "He also had the cooperation of a sympathetic press corps, which even then largely obeyed his instructions not to portray his disability. "No movies of me getting out of the machine, boys," he told photographers as his car arrived at the Hyde Park polling station on Election Day. And, in fact, the cameramen dutifully waited until he had been lifted from his auto and adjusted his braces, whereupon he gladly posed for photos. According to one account, throughout the '20s news photographers actually "voluntarily destroyed their own plates if they showed Roosevelt in poses that revealed his handicap."

The lengths that the Democrats went to dupe the public voting populace, as well as the Republican Party, was incredible *"FDR's Deadly Secret"* continues on page 38:

> ". . . in a dramatic press conference in Albany, during which Dr. E. W. Beckwith, medical director of the Equitable Life Assurance Society, pronounced the governor remarkably fit and announced his company and 21 others had agreed to insure his life for $560,000, payable to the Warm Springs Foundation. "It has rarely been my privilege… to see such a remarkable physical specimen as yourself," declared Beckwith, "and I trust that your remarkable vitality will stand you in good stead throughout your arduous campaign."

With the media and many others enlisted in the efforts to promote the ailing Roosevelt to the Presidency, FDR also enlisted the help of party insiders, promising them political positions and other favors to ensure that he would secure his party's nomination.

He soon had the party's nomination and broke with the tradition of political conventions being attended by delegates alone. He entered the hall to make an unscheduled speech.

There he introduced his New Deal platform which consisted of the reduction of government spending, a sound currency, a balanced federal budget, and an adherence to the US Constitution. He would go on to systematically break every one of these promises. The entire appearance was agenda driven by the need for the party to see how he could "walk."

In the twelve years that followed the Administration of Woodrow Wilson, the Harding, Coolidge and Hoover Presidencies flew by. Harding died mysteriously in office and the low-tax Coolidge economy led to the economic boom known today as the "roaring twenties" and "Coolidge Prosperity."

With the Presidency of Herbert Hoover and the return of stronger government regulations over the country's commercial, banking and business interests, the economy faltered. Hoover encouraged farm cooperatives to hoard grain surpluses and sell the grain only when the prices rose.

This was a catastrophe for farmers and resulted in the bankruptcy of every farm cooperative. Hoover ordered the Federal Reserve to loosen their regulations on credit banking which created relaxed policies at lending intuitions. Such relaxed loan qualifications made it possible for reckless investors to pump credit dollars into the stock market at a frenzied pace.

Margin buying of stocks (putting only 10% down and getting the other 90% in broker's loans) grossly overinflated the market, triggering a massive selloff. That sell off was called the stock market crash of 1929.

Decades prior, Communists had infiltrated the government as well as most of the labor unions which were influencing America's social reformers. They had convinced President Hoover to approve a number of public works projects that would create taxpayer-funded jobs for the unemployed.

Hoover agreed, and the program was put into place. This was Hoover's New Deal, but he would never be remembered for it. Congress soon approved two billion dollars to save the numerous failing banks, lending institutions, and farm cooperatives.

Unemployment rates reaching as high as 50% were commonplace, with many forced to wait in food lines that were established by everyone from national charity organizations to mob boss Al Capone, who flatly refused to let the great people of Chicago starve.

At one time in my family five generations were alive, and real stories of the Depression were passed down to me. My family was one of the lucky ones as they experienced little effect of the economic downturn. In fact, I can clearly remember my grandmother, whose father worked on the railroad, telling me that they had no idea that there was anything wrong.

Nonetheless, the country was in a hideous financial condition as more than 11,500 banks had failed and the nation's banking system on the whole nearly ceased to function. The American experiment of Capitalism and Democracy seemed to have ended as many feared that the country was poised for revolution.

This was the sixth economic depression in the nation's history, and although Hoover had studied the measures necessary to alleviate the economy's woes, he couldn't garner the support of the Democrats for similar remedies. Hoover had the misfortune of being stonewalled by his Congress and went down in history as the least respected president in the 20th Century.

That was a feat that the next president, Franklin Roosevelt, would ride to glory. Spending his entire campaign assassinating Herbert Hoover's character, FDR easily won the presidential election of 1932 and his fellow Democrats swept the elections in both houses of Congress.

The passage of the Twentieth Amendment changed the date in which the president would be sworn in from March to January, but the amendment wouldn't go into effect until October of 1933. This meant that President Roosevelt would have to wait to take office for four solid months.

This allowed him the additional time that he needed to draw up his New Deal, fooling people into thinking that he had done all this work in the now-famous "100 Days."

To this day, newly-elected presidents still try to emulate FDR, as the first 100 days are used as a benchmark of their initiatives, not knowing the origins behind it, or the impossibility of the timeline to really get anything done. During this gap in time the nation's banking crisis had worsened, resulting in President Hoover asking Congress to temporarily close the banks until the monetary system could be stabilized.

When House Democrats blocked his request, Hoover asked FDR personally to support him in averting any potential banking crisis. Roosevelt ignored Hoover, allowing the banking system to collapse so that no Republican could be credited with solving the country's banking crisis. For Hoover, insult came with a huge side order of injury.

American tradition dictated that the outgoing president ride alongside the newly elected president in the same car. Hoover was forced to sit next to Roosevelt in silent humiliation while Roosevelt celebrated before his fellow Democrats. It was quite possibly the dirtiest trick that a president ever played on another, and it resulted in millions of starving people.

During the 2016 Presidential campaign, Donald Trump named Hillary Clinton "Crooked Hillary," claiming that she was the most corrupt politician to ever run for the office. Had Mr. Trump done his political homework he would have found that Franklin Roosevelt could have easily given her a run for her money. FDR has been called the most arrogant, underhanded and the most smug phony ever to hold the office.

Immediately after his inauguration, he called a special session of Congress requesting that his fellow Democrats give him broad executive powers far beyond the scope of what was allowed by the Constitution.

Although not at war, Congress drew upon Woodrow Wilson's 1917 "Trading with the Enemy Act" (TWEA), to grant FDR the power that he sought. The passage of the 1917 Act granted the president the power to oversee or restrict any and all trade between the U.S. and its enemies in times of war. In 1933, FDR's Congress amended the Act by passing the Emergency Banking Relief Act, which extended its scope to include, among other things, outlawing gold ownership.

Through Executive Order 6102, these restrictions were granted and continued until January 1, 1975. The naïve among us would be amazed to learn that the Act has been amended several times since then and that the TWEA remains enacted and in place to this day.

Incredibly, no one in our government has ever, or will ever, tell the public exactly what the Act had been amended to include! That's a move that would have made Colonel House, Woodrow Wilson and Karl Marx very happy. Although he was a very cunning manipulator of the public trust, President Roosevelt's real genius was in his communication.

Using the newest mass media venue of the day, radio, Roosevelt's frequent fireside chats were broadcast into living rooms nationwide. In this way he was able to sell his ideas to his listeners using colorful language and pompous reasoning.

His typical listeners were honest and hardworking people whose demeanor resembled the family in the TV series *The Walton's*. These highly patriotic and loyal families were raised to trust their government and their leader's decisions without question.

It was this common thread within our citizens which allowed FDR to easily enact and sell his New Deal legislation. When FDR started his fireside chats, American propaganda was born. The New Deal legislation was an explosion of social programs designed to put the masses to work in a fashion that any Communist dictator would have been extremely proud of.

These actions offered hope and restored the faith of the American people in transforming the federal government into an instrument of social justice. As global Fascism and Communism flourished, FDR adapted their principles to further the work of Woodrow Wilson.

According to PBS:

> "Roosevelt felt it was the federal government's duty to help the American people weather these bad times. Together with his "brain trust," a group of university scholars and liberal theorists, Roosevelt sought the best course of action for the struggling nation. A desperate

Congress gave him carte blanche and rubber-stamped his proposals in order to expedite the reforms. During the first 100 days of his presidency, a never-ending stream of bills were passed, to relieve poverty, reduce unemployment, and speed economic recovery."

It's amazing how some things never change. Today some university professors still believe that they have all the answers to the nation's ills and continue to voice them and pound their opinions in the ears of their students. This is a less-than-desirable event for those students who have paid multiple thousands of dollars for an education, not to hear opinions somewhat less than connected to coursework.

College professors' entire lives are taxpayer funded and live in an insulated bubble. They have no experience in making profits or paying overhead, yet they continue to pass along open-ended theories with no experience of practicality.

Starting at preschool and ending with their graduate degrees, they never leave their padded world and they don't exist in the universe of brow beating the bottom line, having to grow their customer base, or having to generate profits. Nonetheless they continue to be put in governmental leadership roles, and when they fall short of their lofty expectations people are shocked. Why?

A perfect example of this is happening in New York State at this very moment where Governor Andrew Cuomo has fathered a "START-UP NY" program. According to their website they offer ". . . new and expanding businesses the opportunity to operate tax-free for 10 years on or near eligible university or college campuses in New York State partnering with these schools gives businesses direct access to advanced research laboratories, development resources and experts in key industries."

Forbes.com reports the following:

> "The state of New York, which lost 122,000 private sector jobs last decade, has botched its latest attempt to subsidize growth. After months of foot-dragging, the Empire State Development Corporation released a report last week about Start-Up NY, a program that it began under Governor Andrew Cuomo to attract tech innovation. Despite Cuomo's promises, the report found that Start-Up NY spent millions in marketing dollars, while creating laughably small returns."

> "The report summarized the first year of a program that Cuomo launched in 2014 to create tech clusters in the state, giving tax breaks to tech-related businesses that open near college campuses. The state has already spent $47 million on advertising, and overall public expenditures for the program's first three years are expected to be $323 million. Total job creation figures after five years are expected to be 2,085, but so far that figure stands at a whopping 76 jobs."

Unlike Roosevelt, if I were going to ask someone for business advice, I would ask someone who has been neck-deep in the business world on a daily basis. By the same token if I needed advice about golfing, I would ask Jack Nicklaus, not someone who has been paid to read about golfing but has never golfed. I have nothing against universities, professors or their work; in fact I am very good friends with most of my professors, I am simply stating their strengths and weaknesses.

The fact that Roosevelt hated business and the idea of them making profits and leaned closer to the public unions that controlled the professors, weighed heavily on his decisions. In doing so, President Roosevelt took another page out of Woodrow Wilson's three publications that he had written before he was president.

He gathered a core of university professors who insisted that if they fiddled with legislation the situation could be easily fixed. The following are sixteen pieces of the New Deal Legislation that were enacted as a result of those meetings:

March 10	Emergency Banking Act
March 20	Government Economy Act
March 22	Beer-Wine Revenue Act
March 31	Creation of Civilian Conservation Corps
April 19	Abandonment of Gold Standard
May 12	Federal Emergency Relief Act
May 12	Agricultural Adjustment Act
May 12	Emergency Farm Mortgage Act
May 18	Tennessee Valley Authority Act
May 27	Securities Act
June 5	Abrogation of Gold Payment Clause
June 13	Home Owners Loan Act
June 16	Glass-Steagall Banking Act
June 16	National Industrial Recovery Act
June 16	Emergency Railroad Transportation Act

After this flurry of penmanship, it became very obvious that if you ate, worked, grew a crop, or used utilities, your entire existence was completely controlled by FDR and the federal government. The same could be said for those living under Joseph Stalin in the Soviet Union.

Suddenly the line that separated the two ideologies was almost nonexistent. Although their means of entering office and their methods of practice were far different, the end result was the same: complete and total dominance of their populations.

The parallel between the Soviet Union and FDR's newly concocted America was no coincidence. In fact, it was decades in the making and was ushered in by the Communist Party of the United States of America (CPUSA).

The CPUSA's year of inception was 1919, and they quickly engaged in espionage by infiltrating workers unions, as well as a variety of liberal institutions, using them as front groups. This worked especially well as they became "a presence within the powerful labor federation, the Congress of Industrial Organizations (which would later merge with the American Federation of Labor, to become the AFL-CIO)."

According to www.DiscoverTheNetwork.org, "The Great Depression presented the Party with an opportunity to recruit and build its membership. Thus, the CPUSA used hard times as a propaganda tool to assail the failure of capitalism, targeting particularly the liberal policies of the early FDR administration while successfully infiltrating government agencies, notably the Agricultural Adjustment Administration."

The highly influential and very powerful United States Communist Party has a national office on 235 W. 23rd Street, New York, NY, and their official website is www.cpusa.org for those interested. Their plan was to infiltrate America with their spies and take advantage of their floundering economy.

With Communist operatives and spies working for Stalin in almost every union and progressive organization in America, the knobs and levers of the free world were constantly being twisted and fiddled with. With Roosevelt's New Deal designed and organized by university scholars that were the product of the same academia that Stalin had brainwashed, Roosevelt's New Deal didn't have a chance of working, and it didn't.

By the fall of 1934 the legislation of the New Deal had only a marginal degree of success and produced little more than a sense of hope that someday the country would recover. The economy was a little better, and in that's year's election FDR's Democrats, unaware that their platform had been designed by the CPUSA, had taken majorities in both houses of Congress.

By 1935 Roosevelt was feeling the pressure of the next year's presidential election. He feared that the voters had lost their zeal for his fireside chats. With that in mind, FDR passed new legislation calling for a second New Deal.

It included the Social Security Act, the Works Progress Administration and the Wagner Act. The Social Security Act established an economic "safety net" providing unemployment, disability insurance as well as old-age pensions. The WPA provided the unemployed with work designed to lift their self-esteem.

The Wagner Act created a new independent agency called the National Labor Relations Board (NLRB). This board consisted of three members appointed by, who else, King Roosevelt, and enforced employee rights.

It granted employees the rights to form unions, join unions, and it forced employers to bargain collectively with unions desired by the majority of employees in a workplace. Why was Roosevelt fussing so much over unions? Simple - votes.

That same year the Congress of Industrial Organizations, or CIO, was established. It was a federation of unions that organized workers in industrial unions. The CIO was a staple of the CPUSA and supported Roosevelt and his New Deal policies.

One hand washed the other nicely in the political arena, and with this pairing of votes for favorable union policies the Democrats laid the groundwork for a mutual admiration society that exists to this day between the two. This information has nothing to do with my personal feelings about labor unions. I am merely stating facts.

The same year that Roosevelt was busy "glad-handing" union voters, Adolph Hitler was busy reorganizing the German war machine. A few people within our government knew what was coming and they were vocal, but no one was listening.

With the rise of Nazism, the CPUSA changed its policy and adopted the "Popular Front" tactic. This allowed their operatives to pose as anti-fascist and defenders of American liberalism. The following was taken from the CPUSA website: "This new tactic increased the Party's membership to nearly 100,000 people." In the end, the New Deal proved to be a very costly and largely ineffective chunk of liberal legislation.

To afford the vast expanse of federal spending and federally sponsored work programs, which translated into having a good portion of the United States being supported by the government, Roosevelt completely ignored the recommendations of his generals and made drastic cuts to the United States military.

This enraged every military commander in the country; it was also the same year when Italian dictator Benito Mussolini agreed to form the Rome-Berlin Axis in Europe, setting the stage for the decade of tyranny that followed. Little notice was taken by FDR, as he ignored both his Chiefs of Staff and his generals.

President Roosevelt won his election by a wide and sweeping margin with the support of unions, laborers, farmers, and the poor. With this, he discovered that it was easy to look good spending other people's money, and that you could even buy election votes in the process.

It was a lesson that he would never forget and one that would be passed down through the party. During the celebration the president learned that not everyone in the nation was bending to his will, as the Supreme Court ruled that substantial portions of his second New Deal proposals were unconstitutional.

The Supreme Court was made up of judges, who were not appointed by FDR, who were determined to prevent the merging of the Executive and Legislative branches of the government. So, as Hitler broke the Treaty of Versailles and took control of the Rhineland by military force, FDR focused his attention on appointing more federal judges to tip the scales to favor his legislation.

The outcry from both parties was incredible as they handed Roosevelt his first dose of reality. Six months later as FDR tried to "pack the court" full of his friends so that he could get his initiatives passed, Hitler's army invaded Austria, Czechoslovakia and Poland, which led to the full outbreak of War in Europe. The events that unfolded had proven military leaders like MacArthur and Patton to be correct, but there was still no funding approved for the US military.

As war erupted in Europe, Roosevelt was celebrating the passage of substantial portions of his Second New Deal. Apparently, a little Roosevelt magic was performed on two of the Supreme Court Justices who swung their support from their previous conservative stance, and their votes passed the legislation.

While the Supreme Court scratched their heads as to how that could have possibly happened, FDR was still fiddling with the knobs and levers of the nation. By 1939, Hitler had broken his pact with Stalin and Germany was fully engaged in warfare with the Soviet Union. The world was now viewing Hitler as mentally unstable as he was attacking his country's perimeter at will. Roosevelt did nothing.

Scholars now believe that FDR intentionally delayed economic recovery with his New Deal legislation. Most striking and most recent of these critics came in 2014 in a published work entitled "The Enduring Myth of FDR and the New Deal, Rather than end the Great Depression, his policies prolonged it" by Stephen Moore.

Published in *The Washington Times*, Moore gives the real facts on the damage Roosevelt did to the nation's economy. He writes:

> "The most alarming story of economic ignorance surrounding this New Deal era was the tax increases while the economy was faltering. According to economist Burt Folsom, FDR signed one of the most financially devastating taxes: 'On April 27, 1942, he signed an executive order taxing all personal income above $25,000 [rich back then] at 100 percent."

Another highly credible blow-by-blow critique came from UCLA, where two economists delved into why the economic lull under the Roosevelt reign lasted for almost 15 years. The article published in the *Journal of Political Economy*, quotes the following:

". . . prices across 19 industries averaged 23 percent above where they should have been, given the state of the economy. With goods and services that much harder for consumers to afford, demand stalled and the gross national product floundered at 27 percent below where it otherwise might have been."

Even the most ardent Roosevelt supporters have trouble explaining his reasoning. Why, after the first New Deal failed, did he push a Second New Deal? The answer to this mystery was hidden in plain sight for all to see in the Communist Manifesto. FDR needed to control the means of production and tried to convince generations of economists that followed not to believe in Capitalism. With his second New Deal the transformation to Communism was complete.

The model that he intended later generations to follow was one of no wealth, complete governmental control, and enforced poverty all wrapped up in a *cradle-to-grave* system. The 1936 Rome-Berlin Axis was strengthened by the signing of the "Pact of Steel" which bound fascist Italy and Nazi Germany together.

This was now a full military alliance. Mussolini assisted Nazi Germany in annexing the Sudetenland, and entered the war on the Axis side. Germany and Italy were now partners in war. While America's free market economy was dying a slow death, the British Prime Minister, Winston Churchill, began his communication with President Roosevelt regarding Hitler's intentions.

Churchill, who had recently been made Prime Minister after the failings of Neville Chamberlain, knew what was coming, and within a short amount of time saw his country engulfed in flames. In June of 1940, Mussolini declared war on Britain and France, and FDR finally understood that the war was much bigger than just a European conflict. England, our greatest ally, was in serious trouble as Hitler began to unleash an aerial assault

Although that started the aerial hostilities, Hitler's full wrath fell on Britain between August and November. On September 7, 1940, Hitler launched an aerial pounding of London that he thought would force England into submission and a timely surrender, but he gravely miscalculated the resilience of the English people.

For 57 consecutive nights Hitler pounded the English from the air as nearly 40,000 people were killed and more than a million houses were leveled. The bombs that were dropped on the city and the surrounding areas forced its citizens to take cover in the "tubes" (the English name for subway system) as droves of men, women, and children were sent fleeing through the rubble, choking on smoke as flames soared into the sky.

Lucky to be alive, they huddled for days, sitting ducks, hearing the bombs bursting over their heads as the walls shook and tiny pieces of concrete and dust rained down upon them. They had no way to know where the next bomb would land, on one of their houses "up top" or directly on their heads.

Another city that was on the receiving end of Hitler's massive air raids was Coventry. Coventry was repeatedly bombed on November 14, 1940, by more than 500 German bombers.

In looking for an eyewitness to these events I didn't have to look very far. When my Grandfather's brother, who I called Uncle Howard, was wounded in the Battle of Saint-Lo he was transferred to a military hospital near Coles Hill, England.

There he met the love of his life, a local woman, who soon became his bride. After the war she would leave Britain to begin her family with her new husband in the United States, but not before living through the hell that was Hitler's air raids. It is unfortunate that the Lord took my Uncle Howard from us in 2001. He, like all of my Grandfather's brothers, was a terrific person. He received a Purple Heart and the Bronze Star for his heroics in combat.

As luck would have it, both he and his bother Bob landed on Normandy Beach during the battle that would later come to be known as D-Day. Amazingly, both survived the blood bath. The Lord took my Uncle Bob from us in 1984, and like Howard he also received the Purple Heart for his fighting in France. I hope wherever the heavens have placed them they are aware of the fact that I am writing this book to commemorate their bravery.

We were a close family who lived in a small town, but in all the years that we had those two brothers, no one ever had a memory of them talking about the war. It was obvious that the pain of those memories was too great for them to recall, and neither of them wanted to relive the horrors that they had left behind.

This was also the case for Howard's wife, Joan. It took Joan seventy-four years to be able to speak with someone about the air raids that she had survived, and that someone was me. I just love my Aunt Joan, who is now ninety-seven years old and remains completely independent.

She is jovial and kind and still speaks with a very distinct English accent. She is a wonderful addition to our family and has a few qualities that I wish I had in abundance. The following is her eyewitness account about surviving Hitler's air raids.

How old were you then?

Joan: *It was 1940, so I was 17.*

You were born in Coles Hill?

Joan: *No, I was born in Birmingham and then we moved near Coles Hill. We were in between Coventry and Birmingham and that was a bad place to be [chuckling].*

You're lucky to be alive!

Joan: *I have had some close calls. There were some bombs in my backyard.*

What?! There were bombs in your back yard?!

Joan: *Yes. Incendiary bombs, they started fires. There was a boy up the street who came and he had a shovel and he started hitting one of them. It exploded and he went blind. He was young, you know, a teenager.*

What did the government do to protect you?

Joan: *Well the first thing they did was put up the balloons, you know, the barrage balloons. They were all over.*

What balloons?

Joan: *They were huge balloons that were supposed to catch planes. They were huge things. There was one that was close to where we lived. They were put up by the army units to help stop the bombings and screw up the planes.*

How did it affect you guys when you were just kids?

Joan: *Well, I was older. My brothers were all younger though.*

How did it affect them, did they just go and play like usual?

Joan: *Yeah, they went to school and everything. We would always get under the stairs if we were home and there was an air raid. That was supposed to be the safest. There was a blackout always. You couldn't use lights at night. The cars at night, they had things over the lights, the headlights, so from the air you couldn't see them.*

You guys must have been terrified.

Joan: *Not really. It became normal after a while and you got used to it. We would go outside sometimes and watch the flames, you know, during the raids. There was a searchlight up at the top of the hill. That was the army too but you could see the searchlight and the planes caught in them, you know. There were big guns up there too. When those guns fired the house really shook.*

Were they anti-aircraft guns?

Joan: *Yeah they were —"ack ack" guns were what we called them. We saw Coventry burn. We were standing outside and we had our helmets, of course, and it lit up the whole sky bright red. You could tell if they [German planes] were loaded with bombs because they sounded different.*

How did they sound different? Were they louder when they were loaded?

Joan: *It's hard to describe. I can't describe it really. The sound they made wasn't steady; it was more of an uum, uum, uum sound. They sounded different than our planes, the ones I was building.*

You built planes??! [laughing]

Joan: *Yeah, my Spitfires.*

[laughing]. . . what was your job?!

Joan: *Oh I did everything, sheet metal work and all kinds of things.*

Did you ever get bombed?

Joan: *Yeah, we did. One time we couldn't get out because of the big hanger doors, and the planes were flying so low and they were shooting. You couldn't get out to the shelter, you know. It was all glass inside of the big part [of the factory] you know, because that's where they used dope, they called it, to treat the planes.*

The aileron and the elevators, they were fabric. The rest of the planes were metal. That's why they could do what they did. They were far outnumbered but they saved the Battle of Britain because they out maneuvered the German planes. They were made of Duralumin. It must have been some kind of lightweight aluminum.

We had a bomb land so close to us one day that windows on the factory all bulged in but didn't break. The foreman was really mad at us because we ran back in the factory to get our shoes, because they were so precious. If you had shoes, you know you took them to work and they were a really precious thing.

> *There had to be food rations and all kinds of things.*

Joan: *Oh yeah, there were. We had coupons. Stamps they were, in fact. I think you got two eggs a week. I can't remember what else [the rations were]. . .*

> *Thank god for Churchill.*

Joan: *He came to where I worked to look at the planes and gave us the "V sign" for victory.*

What was he like?

Joan: *He just looked grumpy you know, the same as he always did. Eleanor Roosevelt visited too. She had a run in her stockings and one of the girls ran up to her and gave an extra pair. [laughing]*

Winston Churchill was really a fantastic leader.

Joan: *Oh I think he was.*

Was he popular in Britain?

Joan: *Oh yes.*

How did they ever vote him out of office?

Joan: *I don't know, I was over here then [the United States] and I wondered, I couldn't believe it either. He was smart. He seemed to know what was going to happen ahead of time.*

I can't believe that they voted him out of office.

Joan: *I couldn't believe it either, after all he had done, and then they did that, you know.*

Tell me about Neville Chamberlain. Was he popular?

Joan: *I don't think so. People didn't really like him. They thought he was a milquetoast. He wasn't good. Thank God for Churchill! [laughing]*

It's so great that Britain was able to withstand that pounding. I think Hitler thought that you were like the French. I don't think that the French had that same fighting spirit.

Joan: *I don't think so, because he rolled right over them, and Churchill said we won't do that. We will never surrender. They never thought that we would survive. They were all lined up on the other side of the channel waiting to come in and take us over.*

It's hard to project to future generations how close Britain came to annihilation.

Joan: *They don't have a clue.*

War-torn and ravaged, the call to arms was swift and powerful as Churchill's Royal Air Force retaliated almost immediately after the smoke cleared. Hitler had a false sense of superiority because he had mowed the French down like grass, and he was in a state of blind overconfidence. The Spitfires that my aunt had helped to build gave Hitler fits.

They had a straight twelve-cylinder engine, and could pivot on a dime at almost 400 MPH. In a dive they could achieve speeds over 600 MPH, which was unheard of for their time period. Although the British were outnumbered, the Nazis had nothing that could match this fighter.

Hitler watched in dismay as the Spitfire dominated the Messerschmitt in every contest. All the while, America's worst nightmare was slowly coming true; Germany and England were fully engulfed in war. FDR, always the media spin doctor, understood that it was only a matter of time before the Americans would be sucked into the war, but there was an election looming and he didn't want to stir public sentiment against his candidacy. Although he outwardly preached neutrality to the voters and conveyed the message of separation from Europe's war, he did everything possible to provoke the Axis into attacking America. This was masterfully played by FDR. He supplied ships and munitions to the enemies of the Axis with a "Lend-Lease" program which boosted the US economy before his election to ensure his victory.

Retaliating against the Lend-Lease program, German U-boats attacked merchant ships in the Atlantic. Hungary and Romania both joined the Axis Powers, and Italians began to invade Egypt. The war was spreading out and it was obvious that this was not just "Europe's war" anymore. While FDR was supplying the Allies with ships and supplies he was also doing everything in his power to provoke the Japanese into war as well.

These events are well covered and explained in a timeline written by former US President Herbert Hoover. In Herbert Hoover's book, entitled *History of the Second World War and Its Aftermath*, is proof positive that FDR and his advisors misled the US population about their peaceful intentions.

He writes:

> "Consider Japan's situation in the summer of 1941. Bogged down in a four-year war in China she could neither win nor end, having moved into French Indochina, Japan saw herself as near the end of her tether. Inside the government was a powerful faction led by Prime Minister Prince Fumimaro Konoye that

desperately did not want a war with the United States."

Without a response from the American government to negotiate, and starving for natural resources, the current Japanese government fell and the new regime had no choice but to be hostile to the United States. Desperately seeking answers to their country's problems, they joined the side of America's enemies creating the Tripartite Pact.

This pact was signed by Germany, Italy and Japan creating a very formidable Rome-Tokyo-Berlin axis. Europe's war was no longer limited to Europe, and the location of Imperial Japan was dangerously close to America's territories in the south Pacific.

The Philippines and Hawaii were now in serious risk of attack, and FDR knew it. Despite his economic shortcomings, Roosevelt was an excellent war president. In this venue his cunning and zeal for strategy were at their very best. He knew that if the country were attacked he could sell the war to the American people and look like a hero in the process.

Although I could find no document in the national archives that *directly* said that FDR knew a Japanese attack on the United States was coming, several documents discussed it and even hinted towards it. With that said, we must be reminded of what the national archives are. The national archives are not the gate keeper of truth, or the container of all knowledge great and small. The national archives are a fancy name for the library of government stuff, and you can only see what is provided for you.

In a sense, it's like a Facebook page. You can't see photos that you aren't given permission to see, but it doesn't mean that those photos were never taken. Could documents have been withheld for submission to the national archives to protect FDR?

Judging from the way the press covered up his handicap, the way his party got an insurance company to lie about his physical prowess, and how history books continue to paint him as flawless, nothing would surprise me. In fact, in my mind, that's exactly what happened, and it wouldn't be the first time.

On November 22nd, 1963 President Kennedy was gunned down and the FBI had asked Special Agent in charge of Dallas, Don Adams, to do the unthinkable. Count the number of shots, take and log photos of the bullet holes, and organize them into a report for his superiors. This is further explained in my book *Who Murdered JFK?*

Adams did as he was instructed, finding evidence of eleven shots. Decades later, when he went to write his book on the assassination, none of the evidence that he had personally logged could be found in the national archives, but they do exist. The point that I am laboring to make is that there are no national archive of a man's personal thoughts, and when national security is on the line strange things happen to documents that don't fit the promoted narrative.

In fact, non-governmental parties who wish to have their books or other submitted material archived must apply and pay a fee for consideration. It's an expensive and long process that often ends in disappointment. In fact, in all the people that I know who have tried, only one person was successful, and he ended up being contacted by the FBI regarding the content.

In the case of Pearl Harbor, what is clearly stated in the national archives is that British and American intel communities had clearly broken the Japanese communication codes months before the Hawaiian attack. They knew exactly what as going on.

Beyond having to sell the war to the voters there were other factors at play. British intelligence officers had also supplied information, through Churchill, about a devastating new weapon that the Nazi were very close to unleashing. That weapon was the Atomic Bomb.

FDR knew that the attack on Pearl Harbor was necessary, and that America needed to enter the war immediately. If they delayed, the Nazis would have had time to finish their heavy water experiments, and with their V2 rockets to carry the atom-splitting bombs to every Allied country, Germany would have ruled the world.

FDR knew that it was imperative that America enter the war as soon as possible. If he delayed, millions upon millions of innocent people would have been senselessly murdered with the entire globe completely dominated by one ruler: Adolph Hitler.

It was a sleepless night for the President as the weight of the free world was on his mind. He knew the enormity of what was coming. As he sipped coffee in the hallowed rooms of the White House the silence was deafening. No president since Lincoln knew what this felt like. With a heavy mind he ran through the different scenarios of both his public and military response.

Few people in the United States of America knew where Pearl Harbor, Hawaii was, and even fewer could find it on the map, but within the next 12 hours that would rapidly change. As dawn broke on the 7th of December, it marked the end of a horrific and sleepless night of mental torment. President Roosevelt's temples were pounding, and his eyes were burning as the top brass of his military arrived.

One by one, just like clockwork (and as instructed the day prior), they marched into the war room with serious faces. They knew that the only thing left to plan was the response. Their faces were etched with lines and wrinkles that didn't seem to be there the night before.

FDR had them working overtime and they were as exhausted as he was. FDR's special military advisor, and Chairmen of the Joint Chiefs of Staff, Admiral Leahy, was the first man through the door. Of all the military pillars at this meeting, he was the bigwig. Nothing happened without his permission.

He answered only to the President. He wanted to spend the night at the White House so he could be there at first light, but Roosevelt sent him home. He was looking haggard and the President wanted him to get a solid night's rest "in your own bed." Against his will, Leahy did what he was told.

The next through the door were General George Marshall, who was the Chief of Staff of the Army, and Admiral Ernest King, who was the Commander of the entire US naval fleet. The two men lived near one another, and the driver sent to get the men brought them both in the same car.

Five minutes later General Henry Arnold arrived. Hap Arnold, or "Happy" as FDR called him, was the Chief of Staff of the Air Force. Leahy was focused intently on his pocket watch, almost as if he needed to take attendance. Finally, everyone was there.

The four pillars of our military seated themselves in their usual places in the War Room, but it was not the War Room we know today. Today that room is known as the Map Room. It's a casual room where the first family would sit to visit with dignitaries.

Located on the ground floor of the White House (and just to the right of the Diplomatic Reception Room), the Map Room was very accessible for the wheeled Roosevelt to conduct his military business. Today the Map Room is adorned with Washington's earliest maps, but during the 1940s the only maps shown there were top secret and war related.

The amount of mental anguish and toil that occurred in that room from 1940 until 1945 was simply incredible. It seems impossible to imagine that such a room isn't roped off in tribute to the military genius that toiled there, genius that saved the world, but instead the space sits lost to its glory and largely forgotten. Amazingly, it's just an ordinary room now, a worthless empty shell unbefitting of such important history.

You may think that discussing the free world's fate in a room on the ground floor and next to open windows to be foolish by today's standards, but there was little choice at the time. The construction of the Situation Room wasn't commissioned until the Kennedy Administration twenty years later.

The East Wing wasn't added until the following year when FDR commissioned the construction of an emergency underground bunker complex, and the West Wing was nothing more than temporary office space erected on the parcel where the stables and the greenhouses once stood. In this time period the White House was less of a show piece and more of a utilitarian building: business only, no frills. FDR liked it that way.

As light began to glint through the tall window panes, the men fidgeted. They were uptight and nervous. The day that they had planned for, and dreaded, was about to unfold. They knew that the loss of life was going to be great, and it gnawed at the linings of their stomachs.

They would have given anything not to let this happen, but they knew that it must. They rubbed their eyes and their temples, none of them had slept well, if they slept at all.

Leahy again became transfixed on his timepiece. Although he was silent, his actions screamed: "Where the hell is Roosevelt?!" The men waited impatiently. General Marshall's eyes burned, and he placed in his hand across his face and began rubbing his closed eyelids.

After a few minutes of fumbling to ready their documents, they heard a slight squeak in the distance. It was a squeak that they had heard ten thousand times before. It was the sound of the President's wheelchair, and it was growing closer.

In what seemed like the blink of an eye, FDR appeared. The men were shocked by his pale complextion and his angst. His cigarette holder clinched between his teeth seemed to be taking the brunt of his aggression. FDR greeted them upon his arrival, "Good morning gentlemen." His voice was raspy and his cordial greeting was halfhearted.

He wheeled his chair into his spot at the head of the table and snarled; "OK, let's get started. If we have to be here all goddamned day let's get something in our bellies." As he reached to call for his secretary a different phone rang.

It was the phone that was only used for emergency purposes; it was the "hot line" as FDR called it. A hush fell over the men; their stomachs would have to wait. "Already?!!", FDR blurted. The president was shocked. He answered the phone with haste and listened to the news.

The men were wide-eyed and eagerly waited for the president's details. They were not at all surprised by the attack, but they were surprised by the time of day. In the two minutes that followed the president learned that the Japanese had attacked Pearl Harbor as planned. This was no surprise, but what he heard next was.

He learned that hundreds of planes were involved in the raid. He was visibly shaken. That was something that he wasn't expecting to hear, and being a former Navy man he became angry. The president spoke only a few words into the phone: "How many dead?" When the answer came back that death toll could be in the thousands, he flew into a rage.

Then the phone went dead. A second wave of Japanese fighter planes had made their way to the base and another wave of bombings was underway. They all expected an attack but no one expected this! Three hours later the "hotline" rang again. Finally, the bombing campaign had subsided, and the full brunt of the attack could be tallied and reported. The totality of the attack left 18 naval vessels destroyed or crippled.

The USS Arizona, USS Oklahoma, USS California, USS West Virginia, USS Utah, USS Maryland, USS Pennsylvania, USS Tennessee and USS Nevada were either sunk or heavily damaged. All were burning and thousands of soldiers and civilians had lost their lives.

As the tranquil lagoon in the island of Oahu was transformed into a horrific scene of twisted metal and burning wreckage, the war room erupted into a flurry of activity and Roosevelt readied himself for his public address.

The Japanese, who intended to occupy the harbor and use the base as a launching point to conquer more islands of the South Pacific, intentionally left the onshore facilities intact. The oil storage tanks, shipyards and even the docks were left undamaged as the surgical strike unfolded.

The random elements in this attack were the aircraft carriers that were mysteriously missing that day in the harbor thanks to Admiral King. King had the foresight to order them out of the area to keep them from harm. Battleships were expendable in a retaliatory strike, but aircraft carriers were not.

The Japanese assumed that the entire fleet was at the base and that everything was destroyed. They were wrong. Thanks to the quick thinking of admiral King the U.S. Navy was able to quickly rebound and the result was not in Japan's favor. History.com recounts the events this way:

"After the Pearl Harbor attack, and for the first time after years of discussion and debate, the American people were united in their determination to go to war. The Japanese had wanted to goad the United States into an agreement to lift the economic sanctions against them; instead, they had pushed their adversary into a global conflict that ultimately resulted in Japan's first occupation by a foreign power."

As the greatest orator this country had ever seen made corrections to his speech, he replaced the words *"a day which will live in world history"* with the words *"a day which will live in infamy."*

He knew that changing that word would mean everything. Roosevelt was a genius of annunciation, inflection, and the conveyance of emotion in his speech. He was a natural-born genius of verbal communication, and he knew that this address to the American people would be the most influential that he would ever give.

After his address to the nation, President Roosevelt wheeled himself to the oval office for what he thought would be a few moments to collect his thoughts. Instead he was summoned to the phone. Churchill was already on the line with Admirable Leahy. This conference resulted in the countries of Britain and the United States declaring war on Japan.

Three days later, in a puzzling turn of events, Adolph Hitler declared war on the United States. Finally, the moment FDR had longed for had arrived. America had entered the war and compelled by their feeling of patriotism, droves of men left their families to enlist.

Forty-three days after war had been declared Germany began its U-Boat offensive along the eastern seaboard of the United States. This was done in an attempt to keep America's Navy from delivering its glut of US forces to the European Theater.

Knowing that Japanese, Nazi, and Communist spies were all over Washington, Roosevelt demanded that Japanese-American citizens within the United States be taken to concentration camps. This imprisonment was so illegal that it may as well have torn the Constitution of the United States into shreds.

To Hitler's dismay, American forces arrived in droves and by August the first American air attacks happened in Europe. The war was turning, and it wasn't in favor of the Axis. Soon after, and at the urging of Roosevelt, Churchill made contact with the dictator of the Soviet Union, Joseph Stalin.

Roosevelt knew that the Allies, with the help of the Soviet Union, could pinch Germany between them. With the Allied military advancing from the east and the Soviet military advancing from the west, Germany would be crushed.

Churchill took some convincing because he was horrified by the thought of his country entering a pact with Stalin, but Roosevelt's logic and persistence prevailed. On August 12th 1942, Joseph Stalin agreed to meet with Winston Churchill in Moscow. Churchill knew this would be a difficult encounter, and that Stalin was furious with the Allies.

Stalin believed that the Allies were doing little if anything to help the Soviets as his army faced the German advance across southern Russia. Stalin greatly desired the opening of a second front by the Allies to take the pressure off his Red Army, but despite repeated promises from Churchill, nothing materialized.

Although they put on a show for the camera the two men loathed each other, and Stalin felt misled. Stalin had insisted that the British had promised to launch a second front during 1942, and Churchill once again insisted that no such promise had been made. After formally meeting with no success, Stalin asked Churchill to dine with him in private.

Finally, after so much accusation and personal turbulence, they made a personal breakthrough. Eventually they found common ground and the men parted on friendly terms, but little else was accomplished. Churchill was quick to report the results of his meeting to Roosevelt.

Both understood that Stalin was a puppet master who was capable of magnificent insincerity. They also knew that he was a brutal dictator who had slaughtered tens of millions of his own people.

It was obvious that Stalin not only had an inherent distrust of the western Allies, but his eyes were transfixed on punishing Hitler for his betrayal of the Nazi/Soviet pact. Churchill and Roosevelt worked well together; they trusted each other, and their militaries were on such friendly terms that they formed the Combined Chiefs of Staff (CCS).

The CCS combined the chiefs of staff from both countries as they planned and executed military maneuvers together. No spies existed between these two countries because all of their information was already being shared. The same could not be said for Stalin, whose spy network was as active as Hitler's.

Both countries were being targeted continuously and repeatedly. The Allies remained on friendly terms with Stalin but they viewed him as a temporary ally, much the same way Stalin viewed them. This was discussed at length at the Casablanca Conference in Morocco. This meeting was originally designed to host U.S. President Franklin Roosevelt, British Prime Minister Winston Churchill, and Soviet Premier Joseph Stalin.

FDR was eager to finally meet Stalin, but it was not to be. Stalin turned down the invitation, claiming that the Red Army was too engaged in a major offensive against the Germans to leave them, but that wasn't the real reason. Stalin was sending a message to the two leaders. He was basically saying that if you don't have time to help me and open up a second front, then I don't have time to meet with you. The talk of Stalin, and how to handle him, dominated the meeting.

Roosevelt and Churchill also focused on coordinating a military strategy against the Axis and discussed where such an offensive would take place. The CCS had already examined the map and agreed that the first boots on the ground for the Allies would be in Sicily.

When the conference ended the Allies announced to the world that only an "unconditional surrender" of the Axis powers would be acceptable, and that separate peace treaties with the United States or Great Britain would not be possible.

Seven months after the Casablanca Conference, the Allies began their invasion of Europe with landings on the island of Sicily. The charge was led by British Field Marshal Bernard Montgomery on the southeast and General George Patton from the south. Within four days, nearly 200,000 Allied troops were amassed and were ready to whittle away at the Axis-controlled continent.

Italian dictator Benito Mussolini, who once envisioned rebuilding the Roman Empire to its former glory, watched the control of his country deteriorate and slowly crumble. By March of 1943 there were masses of citizens within the Italian population uniting to overthrow the fascist dictator and join the Allies, but the German military in Italy at that time made any rebellion impossible.

The Allied invasion of Sicily led to the speedy collapse of Mussolini's government, and on July 25th he resigned and was arrested. The next day Pietro Badoglio took control of the Italian government and entered into negotiations with the Allies, becoming their ally. Mussolini was eventually freed from prison by the Germans and reinstated as ruler. With this act the Allies had no choice but to bomb major cities and roll through the landscape.

September and October were horrible months for the Italian people as the Allies invaded the Italian mainland at Calabria and unloaded bombs on Rome. On October 13th the Italians surrendered, joining the Allies and declaring war on Germany for the second time.

Joseph Stalin finally found common ground with the Allies as his spies in America, Italy and Germany all verified that the Allies had kept their word and launched an invasion. Finally, Stalin would be willing to meet with the two Allied leaders; he did so on November 28th 1943, at the Conference in Tehran.

There the three leaders coordinated their military strategy and bickered over what land would be given to what country as Stalin lusted to spread his post-war empire. Stalin wanted a revision of Poland's eastern border and to annex the Republics of Lithuania, Latvia, and Estonia.

Stalin was in the strongest bargaining position as he had been breaking the back of the German army without help for quite some time, and at his instance the British and Americans finally committed to launching Operation Overlord, a mammoth amphibious invasion of northern France in May of 1944.

With that issue settled, Stalin agreed that the Soviet Union would declare war against Japan following the planned fall of Germany. The formation of the United Nations was also discussed at this meeting between Stalin and Roosevelt—without Churchill. This was Roosevelt's day, and he was making it no secret.

FDR wanted what he called "the four policemen" of the globe, who would immediately deal with any alteration of peace with swift action. He wanted those four to be the United States, Britain, China, and the Soviet Union.

Churchill, who had brokered the cooperation between Stalin and the Western Allies, was all but cast aside. Pudgy, round, and rumpled, he sat as a stooge at the meeting while the other two made world plans around him. It was as if he were sitting at the kids table. Churchill was furious.

On June 5th, the Allies entered Rome, and on the following day the invasion that would come to be known as D-Day was launched. One month later than the day they had promised Stalin, the amphibious landing on Normandy had begun. More than 160,000 Allied troops landed along the heavily-fortified French coastline to punch a hole in the Nazi defenses.

The Nazi forces were ready and waiting for the attack. The massive offensive of more than 5,500 ships and 13,200 aircraft supported the invasion and gained a foot-hold in the European continent. By the end of the day's fighting the Allies suffered 9,000 casualties, but their mission was accomplished. More than 110,000 Allied troops punched the necessary hole in Hitler's army and gained their foothold.

Slowly over the next several days they began to cross the European territory held by Hitler's Germany and defeat the Axis. As both tension and desperation mounted in Germany, the fourteenth assassination attempt on Adolph Hitler unfolded.

From Prussia, to Berlin, to Paris, more attempts were made on Hitler's life than on any other military figure in history. Some were random acts of violence, such as attempted poisonings at the Hotel Kaiserhof in 1930. Others were elaborate plans, such as the 20 July plot, Operation Valkyrie, Operation Spark, the Oster Conspiracy, and Operation Foxley.

It was obvious that Stalin, Roosevelt, and Churchill were behind these assassination attempts as the counter-intelligence war between the leaders grew to intense proportions. It can be said in good conscience that long before anyone murdered President Roosevelt numerous attempts were made on the lives of Adolph Hitler, Joseph Stalin, and even Winston Churchill. Amazingly, Churchill's departure would eventually come without firing a shot.

July, August, and September of 1944 saw sweeping victories for the Allies. Soviet troops liberated the first of the concentration camps at Majdanek, the Allied invasion of Southern France began, Paris was liberated, and Finland agreed to a cease fire with the Soviet Union. In October, Allied troops liberated Athens, Greece.

As the war plot thickened, the spy networks on both sides became vivid and entangled. Stalin had spies on Roosevelt, Hitler, Mussolini, Churchill, and even on his own people. Hitler had spy plants in Russia, the US, the UK, and within his own government as well. Churchill had spy rings in Russia, Germany and Italy, while Roosevelt had the luxury of using both the British and Russian intelligence officers.

No leader completely trusted the others, because when it came to war, especially a war of this magnitude, no leader was safe, and assassinations of top military people and their informants were common place.

The last-ditch effort by the German army to establish a success happened in mid-December and lasted well into January of 1945. This offensive was launched in the dense forest and vegetation of Ardennes, a region that covered parts of Belgium, Luxembourg, and France.

The German surprise attack caught the US forces completely off guard, and they sustained heavy casualties. Unfortunately for the Germans, their success came at a very high price. There was a heavy loss of life, and Hitler was never again able to fortify this front to his satisfaction.

The battle would later be named the "Battle of the Bulge" and would go down in history as some of the heaviest fighting of the war, surpassed only by the D-Day invasion.

As Hitler was licking his wounds from this battle, the Soviets captured Warsaw, Poland and liberated the concentration camp in Auschwitz. The victory for the Allied forces was accelerating and in early February, Roosevelt, Churchill, and Stalin met in Yalta.

At their meeting they discussed the need for Stalin to help the US defeat the Japanese, as the Japanese culture would sooner accept complete obliteration than military surrender.

They also discussed the proposed establishment of the UN, the handling of post-war Poland, war reparations payable by Germany and the occupation zone of France. Shockingly, Churchill stated that he didn't see the United States maintaining an armed presence in Europe after the defeat of Germany. This admission shocked Stalin, as it showcased a growing distrust between the two men.

In the end, it was agreed that Germany would undergo demilitarization. German war reparations were to be made in the form of monetary payments (as well as forced labor) to repair war damage. The Polish eastern border was established, Stalin agreed to permit free elections, Roosevelt convinced Stalin to participate in the UN and Stalin agreed to enter the fight against the Japanese. It was also agreed that Nazi war criminals were to be hunted down and tried for their war crimes.

The end of the multi-day conference was marked by a rough draft of the Declaration of Europe's Liberation being signed. Roosevelt saw this situation as being eerily similar to the end of World War I. As Assistant Secretary of the Navy under President Wilson, FDR knew all too well what Wilson had gone through in trying to put a proper end to his war.

Roosevelt knew that very little of Wilson's Fourteen Points were used in the Treaty of Versailles, and that Wilson's failure not only cost him his political career and his legacy but his life as well. Unfortunately for Roosevelt, he would follow in his mentor's footsteps in every possible way.

Neither would have the mental capacity to finish their term in office, nor would they live to see their structures of peace signed. On April 12, 1945, President Roosevelt drew his last breath well short of the assembly of the UN. As the nation mourned his death, the newspaper headlines drew their attention away from what no one would be told. It was rumored that the President's body had turned a mysterious black color within an hour after his death.

The rumor mill both in Washington DC as well as around the world spun out of control. The mystery of President Roosevelt's death and rumors of foul play would only increase as the First Lady refused to let anyone see the body. Sixteen days after Roosevelt's death, Benito Mussolini was captured, shot in the back of the head execution-style, and his corpse was transported to Milan.

There citizens proceeded to kick his face in, spit on his corpse and mutilate his genitals. He and his party were then hoisted in the air and hung by their feet in the center of town where rocks and bottles were hurled at them. This was an Italian message to the world: we will never let this happen to us again. The day after Mussolini was executed, news of Adolph Hitler's death was broadcast.

If anyone naively believes that in a tiny march of days that these events just conveniently "happened," please close the book and call a psychologist. We all know what the history books have told us, but it's what they have not told us that's necessary for all Americans to know.

In doing my research I was most intrigued to learn that FDR's medical records were stolen from a locked safe at Bethesda Naval Hospital shortly after his death and that his internment was the fastest in Presidential history. They buried the most popular president in America (at that time) in less than 69 hours. By contrast, President Lincoln's body was paraded around the country for several days.

The following is from History.com: "On April 21, 1865, a train carrying the coffin of assassinated President Abraham Lincoln leaves Washington, D.C. on its way to Springfield, Illinois, where he would be buried on May 4. The train carrying Lincoln's body traveled through 180 cities and seven states."

Surely a president as popular as FDR deserved a similar sendoff; even President Kennedy laid in state longer as they extended hours so more than 115,000 mourners could pay their respects.

Why is it that they couldn't get President Roosevelt's corpse in the ground fast enough? The obvious answer is that the First Lady had been told that there was more to the story. What Eleanor didn't know was that by burying the president that fast she was helping to cover the tracks of an assassin.

2
The Discovery

It has been said that a journey of a thousand miles begins with a single step. If that is indeed the case, then this journey must start right here. It's up to us to sift through the morsels of history that have been overlooked, ignored, and just plain hidden.

The main event that lies at the core of this period in history is the mysterious death of President Roosevelt. The purpose of this chapter is to provide a chronicle of what the history books have said so that in the next chapter we can challenge and even poke holes in this widely circulated version.

President Franklin Roosevelt died on April 12th,1945. His deteriorating health initially began in 1921 as he was stricken by Infantile Paralysis, a disease later to be named polio. The disease initially paralyzed him from the neck down, but after months of intense determination and physical training his upper body strength and mobility was regained.

The mysterious disease that overtook FDR's body came suddenly and would never leave as his legs would remain paralyzed and useless to him for the rest of his life. It was to his benefit that his family was extremely wealthy and, living less than a mile from the Vanderbilt mansion, could marshal many upper echelon contacts to solicit the help of doctors from all around the world.

Although there was no helping Roosevelt regain the use of his legs, one of the doctors suggested that he regularly visit Warm Springs, Georgia. There, in the soothing waters, FDR could use his legs to exercise while he was weightless in the pool. He loved Warm Springs, and while he has there he met many others suffering from the same disease.

He particularly took to the children who were also stricken, and formed a close bond with their families. For the first time in his life he knew what it was like to be disadvantaged. It was out of this struggle that he determined that the government should be the cradle-to-grave caretaker of the population.

With an ironclad determination he managed to rebound politically, but without the use of his legs. The useless limbs became atrophied, and withered to the diameter of his arms. To deceive the crowds into thinking that he was a physically fit and active man, he attended public appearances and political rallies while wearing steel leg braces that were custom made.

These braces enabled him to lock his legs in place and, with the use of a cane in one hand and grasping the arm of a minion with the other, he was able to give the appearance of good posture. Eventually he was able to train himself to take a few steps on his own before his massive political rallies, but in reality, his legs were limp and they would remain that way.

Rebounding through the awful ordeal of paralysis, he won the Governorship of New York, became Assistant Secretary of the Navy, and went on to win the Presidency of the United States in 1932. Despite his paralysis it appeared that he was returning to his virile ways of the past.

Although he enjoyed reasonably good health throughout his three terms in office, 1943 marked the beginning of the Tehran Conference and the end of President Roosevelt. This conference was a meeting of the Allied leaders. It was there that FDR, British Prime Minister Winston Churchill, and Soviet Premier Joseph Stalin put their minds together to formulate military involvement and discuss their strategies to defeat the Axis powers.

Ending on December 1st 1943, the Christmas holiday was dismal for the President as his health waned. Battered from his public service and war-torn from the pressures of leading the nation through three catastrophic events—the Great Depression, the war in Europe and the war in the Pacific—the courageous leader sought an unprecedented fourth term. While in ill health, the devoted Roosevelt won his reelection in 1944.

His fourth inaugural speech was abnormally brief and was delivered by a man who had no visible energy. This was a stark contrast from the famously verbose Roosevelt who previously opted to take the oath of office from the balcony at the White House rather than the customary Capitol building.

The speech, only four short paragraphs in length, served as a notice that his days of belting out elongated and swaggering orations were finished. Throughout 1944, Roosevelt's health would continue to mysteriously rebound and then, to the dismay of his team of doctors, falter.

In late March of 1944, Dr. Howard G. Bruenn, a naval physician and cardiologist, examined the President and determined that he was suffering from cyanosis, breathlessness, left ventricular enlargement, an apical systolic murmur, hypertension/hypertensive heart disease, congestive heart failure, cholecystitis and bronchitis.

It is needless to say at this point that the President's health had become a mess. With dark sunken circles surrounding his eyes, combined with a weight loss of 40-50 pounds, his clothing hung on him as though he were a scarecrow.

He looked like a ghoulish caricature of his former self and people were starting to take notice. Compounding his hideous appearance was the fact that his hands shook violently, and he had trouble using them effectively.

His shaking would prove to be such an impediment that he would frequently knock over coffee cups, water glasses and even struggle to do the simplest of things such as light his cigarettes or feed himself. He was also developing habits that were very odd.

He would smoke continuously, but rarely finished cigarettes, and his mental capacity seemed to wane as well. He frequently acted as if he were in a daze; his mouth would gape open before his guests and he began calling objects by the wrong words. The public as well as his physicians were baffled.

As the calendar welcomed 1945, the President was dreading the 18,000-mile round trip meeting with his Allied counterparts. On February 4, 1945, FDR attended the Yalta Conference meeting with British Prime Minister Winston Churchill, and Soviet Premier Joseph Stalin.

Roosevelt's appearance shocked the foreign leaders and their aides so much that they claimed that he was a dead man walking. According to one report, Churchill's personal doctor, Lord Moran, claimed that FDR had "only a few months to live." When the Conferences ended on February 11th everyone at that meeting knew that they would never see President Roosevelt alive again.

As February 1945 drew to a close FDR looked like hell; nonetheless, he prepared to address Congress. On March 1st, the President appeared in Congress for the first time in over two years. He was physically, mentally, and emotionally drained.

He was weary from his elongated journey back to the states as well as being drained from the demands of his office. What may have been most shocking is that he stopped trying to conceal his disability.

Roosevelt's intention for addressing the joint session of Congress was to inform the members of our government what had transpired during the conference in Yalta, but what shocked them more than the news of how the Allies were planning to divide up the post war world was the fact that he was seated and remained that way. He publically apologized for his seated position saying that he found it nearly impossible to wear his heavy braces.

The Roosevelt Presidential Library notes the words that he began his speech with: "I hope that you will pardon me for this unusual posture of sitting down during the presentation of what I want to say, but I know that you will realize it makes it a lot easier for me not to have to carry about ten pounds of steel around on the bottom of my legs."

You could have heard a pin hit the floor. The result of him uttering these words was silent shock. This was the first time that he had ever publicly acknowledged his physical disability. His reasoning for this statement was sound. With both his life and his political career at an end, showing them the wizard behind the curtain could no longer harm him.

During the speech the president was a mental mess as he stumbled through his address. He had a terrible time staying on point and lost his place in the speech many times. He disguised his confusion by ad-libbing words and even sentences and eventually used his finger to mark the spot on the paper so he could recover his place.

It became obvious to onlookers that he had some variety of mental impairment. While no one could agree on the cause of his issue, everyone agreed that the great orator of the previous years was no more. FDR's doctors were clueless as to why he couldn't follow the speech or use his eyes properly.

Authors Steven Lomazow and Eric Fettmann tried to explain Roosevelt's health issues in their 2011 book entitled, *FDR's Deadly Secret*. In the book they assert:

> ". . the problem was not with the president's eyes, but with his brain. He was suffering from a neurological condition called left hemianopia, characteristic of a specific focal dysfunction in the right posterior portion of the brain. The errors Roosevelt made present the strongest evidence that a large pigmented lesion over his left eyebrow, which had grown and darkened over a period of nearly two decades, was not a harmless sunspot, but rather a deadly melanoma, or skin cancer."

They continued to speculate that it had become malignant and had metastasized in his brain, creating a tumor that had not only taken his reading skills and eloquence as an orator, but would soon take his life as well.

It is an interesting theory to say the very least, and one that I will revisit in the chapters that follow. Soon after his address to Congress the President was in dire need of rest and there was only one place that he wanted to go, Warm Springs, Georgia.

FDR was looking forward to a few weeks of relaxation and being visited by some friends while he pondered the impending fall of Germany and inevitable rebuilding of Europe. Roosevelt loved Warm Springs as much as his homestead in Hyde Park, NY, and called it the "Little White House." It was his home away from home.

He loved the people and the natural surroundings of Warm Springs so much that he visited there more than fifteen times during his presidency, staying for weeks at a time and always leaving rejuvenated. He was hoping that this trip would be the elixir for his ailments, as it had been so many times before.

On March 30, 1945, FDR's train pulled into the station at Warm Springs, Georgia. The time was 1:33 in the afternoon. As Roosevelt waved to the onlookers his appearance was horrifying. He was noticeably frail in stature, grayish in color and his weakness was all too obvious.

As they were struck by the reality of his illness, an uneasy murmur crept through the crowd. Traveling with the President were his personal friends, aides, relatives and his most trusted confidants as he melted away in the silence and rest of seclusion.

Joining him were his correspondence secretary Bill Hassett, his personal secretary Grace Tully, Tully's typist Dorothy Brady, switchboard operator Louise Hackmeister, two Secret Service agents, his personal Valet Arthur Prettyman, FDR's longtime friend Basil O'Connor, Canadian Ambassador Leighton McCarthy, FDR's cardiologist Lt. Cmdr. Howard Bruenn, and his two favorite cousins; Daisy Suckley and Polly Delano. Eleanor, who did not care for Warm Springs, remained in Washington tending to her busy schedule. They had thought that the President just needed a few days of rest and relaxation and that he was worn down by his many responsibilities to the nation. They were about to get a wakeup call.

Easter 1945 fell on Sunday, April 1, and the stricken Roosevelt looked ghastly in his appearance at the Easter church service. His mannerisms were noticeably odd as his famous gregarious spark was missing. To the dismay of the public, he was stoic and all but avoided greeting the townspeople after the service.

Back at the "little White House," he avoided his presidential duties, stayed out of the warm swimming pools which traditionally soothed his past afflictions, and turned down those requesting visits. The once charming and vibrant Roosevelt who embraced the public and thrived on his love affair with the common people had been reduced to the silhouette of a sickly recluse sleeping for days on end.

His ultimate goal was to regain his strength which would allow him to arrive in the upcoming conference in San Francisco where the charter meeting of what would become the United Nations would be held. After three days of being bedridden, FDR rose like a lion, with strength and vigor that his subordinates viewed as a sign that he was restored to his former self, but by lunch his strength would wain and he would retire seeking more rest.

Dr. McIntire lived under the delusion that if he fattened the President up by administering medicine that would increase his appetite, FDR would somehow return to normalcy. A solid week had passed with no improvement to the president's failing health, or to his dismal spirits, until company arrived. On April 9th FDR received a visit from possibly his favorite person—Lucy Mercer.

Mercer was a woman who was having a multi-decade affair with the president. It was well known by all the White House insiders that in 1918 Eleanor Roosevelt discovered love letters and other correspondences between the two and threatened to divorce him, insisting that he never see her again.

Fearing that the impending divorce would ruin his political career, he agreed. Two things never happened after that day: FDR and Eleanor would never again be passionate or loving toward one another, and FDR would never write another love letter. But the affair continued.

By his inauguration in 1933, the affair was again in full swing as FDR and Eleanor developed more of a professional relationship than a personal one. To the rest of the country the Roosevelts were the personification of a power couple, but insiders knew that the real first lady was Lucy Mercer.

On this trip Mercer had a surprise for her lover; the much anticipated second Presidential portrait was going to be painted. To perform the deed was a woman named Elizabeth Shoumatoff. Shoumatoff was a defected Russian, the "go-to" painter of the American elite, and the same woman who had painted the President's first portrait years prior. Over the next few days as Shoumatoff toiled in vain trying to mask the condition of a man who was grey, sickly and frail in her portrait, FDR and Lucy were going on picnics and enjoying their every minute together.

During the afternoons of Lucy's visit, Shoumatoff was busy studying photographs and making her preliminary drawings. As the days wore on the President had less and less energy to give his guests, and what little he did have was spotty at best.

On the morning of April 11th Shoumatoff was still not entirely satisfied with her selection of poses for the President. That morning she had her photographer, Mr. Robbins, take two more photographs as she probed her mind for options for her project. Listed in this book are the last photographs of Franklin Roosevelt in existence.

As the above photographs were taken, Lucy and FDR chatted happily as the President undertook a reduced work load consisting only of light paperwork and opening mail. The following lunch was joyful and filled with conversation as Lucy, Ms. Shoumatoff, Daisy Suckley, and Polly Delano exchanged stories and pleasantries.

After lunch the President, near exhaustion from his impaired physical condition, retired to his bed and Shoumatoff went directly to work. A short while later she had made her decision on the President's pose and she readied her painting supplies for the next morning's session.

Soon afterward, Mercer and Shoumatoff retired to their guest cottage to freshen up for dinner. That evening, Treasury Secretary Henry Morgenthau was Roosevelt's invited guest for a casual dinner.

Morgenthau joined the President's regular guests; Grace Tully, Dorothy Brady, Louise Hackmeister, Basil O'Connor, Polly Delano, Daisy Suckley, Elizabeth Shoumatoff and Lucy Mercer. Conversation was light and cheerful; however Morgenthau recalled that FDR's hand shook so badly that he found lighting his cigarette and pouring cocktails to be an impossible task.

The affliction was noticed by all who attempted to overlook the President's obvious hand tremors. FDR's charm seemed to temporarily overcome the emotions of the visitors but it was very difficult to do as he kept confusing names at the table.

At dinner the President, who was known for his generosity as well as his hospitality, opened a jar of very rare Russian caviar that Joseph Stalin had given him as a gift as he departed Yalta.

In all of the writings of this event only one person made a formal recollection of Stalin's caviar gift. That person was the Russian, Elizabeth Shoumatoff. Her mention of this event is covered in her book, *FDR's Unfinished Portrait.*

On page 111 she writes, "A big bowl of Stalin's caviar, mentioned by the President on the first night, was served." The gesture was appreciated, but only FDR had acquired the taste of such a high society treat. After the meal, and about an hour of lighthearted chat, the night was cut short as Roosevelt needed to meet privately with Morgenthau as Henry's child was very ill. He managed to summon the strength to have a private meeting before retiring for the night. As the house guests settled in for the night, Mercer and Shoumatoff retired to their rooms at the guest cottage.

Shoumatoff continues: "We were taken to the guest cottage, which was about a hundred feet away from the Little White House and consisted of two rooms. Mine was charming and had a rustic air. It was decorated with reddish toile, with plenty of prints and objects reflecting the president's interest in boats. Lucy's room was light with flowered chintz." As the sun rose on the morning of Thursday, April 12, 1945, so did the heat and the humidity.

By 7:30 am President Roosevelt began his day with neck pain from his slumber. Prior to breakfast he requested a brief massage during his daily examination from Dr. Bruenn. Bruenn, who traveled with the president, had been reporting Roosevelt's medical statistics to his personal physician, Admiral Dr. Ross McIntire, who remained in Washington, D.C. After his examination President Roosevelt readied for his day.

It was going to be an abnormally busy day for the failing president. Posing for his portrait, signing documents, visiting the children who were rehearsing for their upcoming minstrel show, and later in the day attending a barbecue where he was planning to receive his many local friends. All of the events were planned by the townspeople in Roosevelt's honor. The weary President ate a light breakfast and planned an even lighter lunch. He knew that he didn't want to overtax his already-waning appetite.

What he didn't know was that his favorite presidential chef, the cook at the Little White House, was going to surprise him with his favorite dish at the barbecue; Brunswick stew. It wasn't to be. After his breakfast the President immediately returned to his makeshift desk, a card table, to finish dictating correspondences and signing paperwork.

Elizabeth Shoumatoff had set up her easel and arranged the rest of her art supplies in the living room where the president was working. As the artist worked, the president began to tire. After all, it was nearing 1pm in the afternoon and it was way past his naptime, but not wanting to disappoint his guests, the accommodating president was altering his schedule.

While he was working he checked the time and announced "We have got just about fifteen minutes more to work" before they were to eat lunch and prepare for the upcoming barbecue.

As the artist packed up her supplies, FDR's hands shook violently while trying to light a cigarette. The artist noticed the color of his face change from what had been his recent ashen gray to a very healthy color.

It was a transformation that she had noticed all morning and she was thrilled by the development, as it made her job water coloring him much easier. The room was empty with the exception of the artist, and Daisy, who was sitting on the loveseat wrestling with her knitting. As everyone else hurried to assist with the preparation of lunch, the artist packed up her painting supplies and began to fold her easel.

After a draw from his cigarette the president pressed his hands to his forehead and quietly groaned. As the artist exited the room, Daisy noticed that he had dropped his cigarette and was slumped slightly forward.

She mistook the president's distress for him trying to pick his cigarette up from the floor. As she walked over to help him she immediately realized that there was a bigger issue. The president was in horrible condition, as he was only semi-conscious.

"Franklin, what's wrong?" No response. "Franklin?" "Franklin?!" The president, now slipping into unconsciousness, slumped so completely that he nearly fell out of his chair. According to a quote from the book *FDR's Deadly Secret*: "He looked at me with his forehead furrowed in pain and tried to smile. He put his left hand up to the back of his head and said: 'I have a terrific pain in the back of my head.' He said it distinctly, but so low that don't think anyone else heard it-My head was not a foot from his."

Daisy, now frantic, was trying to keep FDR from falling out of his chair while the artist summoned help. Within seconds the room was flooded with people: Arthur Prettyman, Daisy, Polly and a member of the cleaning staff had hastily carried the president into his bedroom.

His extremities were cold, and the smelling salts that had been administered had no effect. His pulse was sporadic and faint. The good coloring of a healthy man that he had displayed earlier had vanished and his complexion was white-gray. He was breathing—barely. His breathing was labored, gravelly and weak.

The women, now hysterical, were fleeing the house and screaming to the Secret Service agents to get help. Dr. Bruenn was snatched from the swimming pool and informed that the president urgently needed his care. Calls were immediately made to Dr. James E. Paullin, FDR's heart specialist in Atlanta, and the President's primary physician Dr. McIntire. The First Lady, Eleanor Roosevelt, was also called.

According to history.com: "(Eleanor) was listening to a piano performance when she was summoned back to the White House. In her memoirs, she recalled that ride to the White House as one of dread, as she knew in her heart that her husband had died. Once in her sitting room, aides told her of the president's death. The couple's daughter Anna arrived and the women changed into black dresses. Eleanor then phoned their four sons, who were all on active military duty."

Meanwhile, back in Georgia, Lucy Mercer was in grave danger of being discovered by the press and was trying to vacate the guest cottage with Elizabeth Shoumatoff as quickly as possible. Could you imagine the scandal if it were discovered that the president collapsed when he was with his longtime mistress while in the company of a defected Russian?

For that, and many other reasons, the two women took the fastest and most secretive route out of Warm Springs. As they pressed the gas pedal to the car's very limits, FDR was barely clinging to life. When the hurried doctor arrived, the president was on his bed and surrounded by frantic people who were sobbing; he immediately cleared the room and shut the door.

FDR's Deadly Secret claims that the doctor found Roosevelt "pale, cold, and sweating profusely" and that "his blood pressure was literally off the charts— 300/190." Dr. Bruenn frantically administered lifesaving measures, but the president's body wasn't responding to the treatments. His breathing became more labored and he began to struggle for each breath.

By now the White House was a beehive of activity as staffers wept uncontrollably and the men in the President's cabinet made the necessary arrangements for Eleanor to fly to Georgia.

As the clock approached 3:30 Eastern Standard Time, the first radio reports began to leak the president's condition to the nation. As the nation slipped into mourning, and the fleeing Mercer came to grips with what she already knew was going to happen, but was fooling herself wouldn't, Eleanor was in flight.

Within in hours she would enter the very room where FDR's mistress had so lovingly attended to his every whim. It wasn't long before Eleanor had been told that Lucy Mercer had been visiting the president for days, and that it certainly wasn't the first time. The two women knew each quite other well.

In fact, Lucy Mercer was Eleanor Roosevelt's secretary in 1914 and assisted her in arranging her social responsibilities and appointments. That's where Mercer caught the President's eye. Eleanor spent some time alone with the body and undoubtedly had mixed feelings. She loved him because they were cousins and they shared a past, but resented him for his betrayal of their marriage and for going back on his word that he would never see Mercer again.

When the First Lady felt as though she had spent enough time with the president's body, she rejoined the others in the living room who were grieving heavily. It has been reported that she was emotionless and "dry-eyed" when she appeared as she consoled the others through their grief.

She had no love left for FDR, only memories of what once was, and those emotions weren't strong enough to bring tears. The Roosevelt family members and dignitaries that had flown to Georgia with the First Lady milled around the house for hours, coming to grips with what had happened, and what needed to happen next. By this time, all three of the president's doctors, Bruenn, Paullin and McIntire, were well-informed of the events and they were in total agreement that no autopsy would take place.

The three of them had successfully convinced the First Lady and many others within the group that an autopsy was a waste of time as they were certain of the cause of death, cerebral hemorrhage.

As the First Lady retired to the guest cottage there remained a swarm of people in the house attending to details and readying the president's body. As Eleanor settled in for the night she could still smell Lucy's perfume in the bedding from the night prior, as there was no time between guests to have anything laundered.

The next day brought the unthinkable task of bringing the president's lifeless body back to the White House where arrangements had already been made for it to lie in state. A military procession in full regalia escorted the hearse down the hill from the Little White House to the train station.

Along the route were soldiers in full ceremonial dress lining both sides of the roadway as a military band played a somber funeral dirge. Amazingly, as would be the case in the assassination of President Kennedy, eighteen years later, the president's body was rapidly taken out of Georgia in violation of Federal law.

Since there was no legally-mandated autopsy performed by a proper state official, the president's body shouldn't have left the state. The laws were the same in Warm Springs, Georgia, in 1945 as they were in Dallas, Texas, in 1963.

This is not just a mistake, or something that the governmental officials overlooked, this was done on purpose. The question is: Why? If there was nothing to hide by having the body autopsied at the state level, then why did someone from within the federal government give this order?

With Roosevelt, as with Kennedy, people on the inside were already starting to ask questions. As Roosevelt's hearse purred down the streets to the train station, onlookers were engulfed with their grief and wept uncontrollably.

To them, President Roosevelt was far more than just a sitting US President, which would have been sufficient enough to warrant their grief, because many of them knew him personally. He visited there so often that they felt as if he were one of their own. Under the most somber and grief-stricken of circumstances, FDR left Warm Springs, Georgia, for the final time at 9:03 am, April 13, 1945.

As the train slowly chugged out of the station onlookers could plainly see Roosevelt's coffin through the windows. It was the most amazing spectacle. Along the railway, tens of thousands of grief-stricken onlookers gathered as the train made its way through the state of Georgia at a speed of 30 miles an hour.

As the train headed north and made its way through the more populated areas of the Carolinas and Virginia, the crowds that lined the tracks increased in both number and depth. Military servicemen both past and present turned out in uniform to offer their final salute to the fallen president.

They stood alongside parents who held infants, small children who were accompanied by adults, and grandparents of all ages and colors. The nation was fully engulfed in mourning the likes of which it hadn't seen since the assassination of President Lincoln eighty years prior.

After finally arriving at Union Station in Washington, D.C. on April 14th, the train was met by President Truman, Roosevelt's immediate family members, and high-ranking officials of the United States Government. There, servicemen placed the flag-draped coffin on the waiting horse-drawn carriage, and the funeral cortège, with all of its pomp and grandeur, proceeded to the White House.

Full military honors were given as the president's funeral procession slowly advanced from the railroad station through the streets of Washington, D.C. Along the route every branch of America's armed forces were present in full military regalia.

Incredibly, the outpouring of sentiment in the nation's capital dwarfed what those onboard the train had witnessed as waves of grieving citizens mobbed the city streets. Businesses closed their doors and the city ground to a grieving halt in what seemed like the longest hour and a half in the nation's history.

After finally arriving at the White House, the casket was placed in the East Room where private mourning was scheduled for only a selected few. Despite numerous requests, the President's casket would remain closed, and there wouldn't be a single soul that would see President Franklin Roosevelt's face ever again.

The Episcopal Funeral services were conducted at 4:00 pm and lasted nearly an hour as there wasn't a dry eye in the city. Some mourned publicly, while others mourned privately, but all were consumed with the loss of their beloved president.

Shortly after the funeral service the casket was removed from the White House by a procession of soldiers and selected policemen headed back to Union Station. There it would begin the 325-mile railway journey to Hyde Park, New York for President Roosevelt's internment. FDR was going home.

The journey on the train was long and tortuous for those who braved the trip with the casket. It was impossible to sleep, as the bumps and shuffles common to rail travel, combined with the loud crowds of mourners along the tracks, made it virtually impossible to get more than a brief nap.

On the morning of April 15th, the funeral caisson arrived at the train station just three miles away from the Roosevelt Mansion, the place that FDR loved so very much. The casket was again loaded aboard a horse-drawn carriage and slowly guided to the Roosevelt estate.

The horses were distracted by the mourners and were misbehaving against the coachman's intentions as the carriage's large wooden wheels nosily navigated narrow roadway. Route 9 in Hyde Park is a beautiful and serene drive, which on that day was cramped with soldiers, sailors and marines giving their final salutes.

The horses were so spooked that some wondered if they would allow the President to return to his boyhood home and his final resting place. Once at their destination, family members, close family friends, neighbors, and limousines containing President Truman and the immediate Roosevelt family assembled themselves for their final goodbye.

Franklin's burial was in the Rose Garden, which was at the extreme right of the mansion. It is the most remarkable place to visit as colorful vibrant flowers of every variety blossom to greet each visitor. Having visited there, it seems completely out of place for such a sorrowful occasion, but it would have been a wonderfully peaceful place to eternally rest.

After a brief reading from the clergy at the St. James Episcopal Church, three volleys were fired into the morning mist. As taps were played, the President's casket was slowly lowered into the ground. An unidentified neighbor remarked that "it was as if the flag itself were crying."

The lush foliage, rolling hills and sparkling waters of the Hudson River was the place that had reared young Franklin into the man that he was. It was the family homestead and the place that he loved more than any other place on earth. President Roosevelt, in every sense of the word, had gone home to eternally rest.

The grave of President Franklin D. Roosevelt at the Roosevelt mansion, Hyde Park NY. Photograph taken by the author on June 8th 2016.

Departing the gravesite were throngs of secret service agents, Roosevelt's personal aides, his family, his White House staffers, his personal valets, and his team of physicians. Aside from their obvious grief, their minds were in turmoil. The physicians were mentally wrestling with the impossible.

How could a patient so radically bounce back and forth between health and mysterious sickness so frequently? Why, during the period of illness, did his body not respond properly to the medicine? An uneasy feeling crept across the minds of the insiders as the doors of the limousines closed and the cars slowly slipped down the elongated driveway.

They would never live long enough to know the truth. When it came to the mystery of President Roosevelt's death, all knew some, but some knew all, and they weren't talking.

Exactly how an extensive probe into the ill-faded medical care of President Roosevelt had escaped the American people's attention immediately after his death is quite beyond me. I can only assume that the public was so preoccupied with not only their grief, but the long-awaited news of the end of the war as well.

The same can be said for the internals of our government, but their attention seemed to have been elsewhere. Despite a few incendiary remarks about Dr. McIntire's medical acumen in the halls of Congress, there was no investigation, and not enough outrage to warrant one.

Fortunately, the father of" Yellow Journalism", Joseph Pulitzer II, was on his toes and sparked public interest in his newspaper, the St. Louis Post-Dispatch. Pulitzer placed his Washington D.C. chief investigator, Pete Brandt, on the case, and ordered him to get some answers. Brandt pressured both Dr. McIntire and Dr. Lahey for interviews, comments, and eventually their full and complete medical records on FDR. Shortly thereafter, a frantic Dr. McIntire wrote Eleanor Roosevelt.

The following is from *FDR's Deadly Secret*:

> "McIntire sent an urgent letter to Eleanor, warning her that Brandt, acting on "a direct order from his publisher," had tried "to secure my permission to publish all the physical and clinical records on the president," he said that "very naturally, I told him that my answer was 'no,' that no good could come of it...
>
> Notwithstanding this, a few days later he called on Dr. Frank Lahey in Boston and asked him to

comment on the president's condition throughout the past year of his life, knowing that Dr. Lahey had been a consultant. Dr. Lahey's reply was much more emphatic than mine." McIntire continued: "You, of course, have the right to say whatever you will care to do about it. But I can see no good coming from such a thing, and moreover, as you have said, the story is closed."

The book continued to question whether the doctor's fear of a subpoena to release the medical files was what led to their disappearance from their safe at Bethesda Naval Hospital. Without question, it had, because at some point shortly thereafter they vanished never to be seen again.

In 1957, Eleanor, who had been hearing continued accusations of physician negligence from friends and family members alike, launched a private investigation into FDR's death. It was only then that Dr. McIntire's dirty little secret was revealed.

When the private investigator, as well as Roosevelt family members, started requesting Franklin's medical files from the Surgeon General's office a dozen years after his death, they were talked around in circles and eventually told the gruesome truth that the files were missing.

Only four people in the world had access to the safe where the files were kept. Dr. McIntire, Captain John Harper (who was the commanding officer of the facility), Captain Robert Duncan, the facilities executive officer, and Thomas Parran, the Surgeon General of the United

States. To add insult to the Roosevelt family's injury, Dr. McIntire would publish a book in 1946 entitled the *White House Physician*. The book, which sold very well, stressed the close friendship between the President and McIntire, and included the doctor's side of the story.

The book, which should have been placed next to Grimm's Fairy tales, defended the doctor's long-running façade that Roosevelt was both well and very healthy right up to his last day on earth. This has got to be one of the biggest conspiracies in American history, and it's one that no one is talking about.

Whatever knowledge the First Lady gained from her investigation into President Roosevelt's mysterious demise wasn't shared with anyone, and less than four years after the investigator's official report was inked she joined her husband in death.

After a two-month battle with a tuberculin disease Eleanor Roosevelt died on Election Day in 1962. If we could reel back the decades, there were thousands of people that we could have interviewed, including the member of the assassination team that Bill Hanson, in his book *Closely Guarded Secrets*, claimed to have spoken with.

As Chapter 2 draws to a close, so does the parochial history lesson of the death of President Franklin Roosevelt. Now it's time to roll up our sleeves and get busy asking some very pointed questions.

3
The Questions

Now that the parochial history lesson of the first two chapters is behind us, it's time to start digging and separate the myth from the reality. Anyone who has read my first book, *Who Murdered Elvis?,* fully understands that repeated stories can be taken as the truth for decades while not really being true at all.

Something horrible has happened to mankind. People have stopped looking for answers, and have started mindlessly repeating what they have been told. Why do people do this?!! I don't know if they are just too lazy to dig into a subject, gather facts and form their own opinions, or if we have become incapable of doing anything more than just rolling over on-command.

Suddenly we have a society full of talkers who don't care to know the truth about anything, they just keep talking. To me this is beyond tolerance. That's where pain-in-the-ass people like me come in handy.

It's my job to dissect what we have been told and tell the whole truth, not just a story that Mother Goose dreamt up for the American public—the real truth. It's my job to unpack and examine decades of publicly repeated crap and make real sense of it.

Telling the world that President Roosevelt died of a cerebral hemorrhage is quite a ballsy claim when there was no autopsy to verify it. That's like looking at the chalk outline of body and claiming to have solved the crime without an investigation. How stunningly stupid to they think the public is?

Yet in every history book there it is: President Franklin Roosevelt died of a cerebral hemorrhage. To further prove my point, there was no embalming, and despite the repeated claims, there was no public viewing of the body. This was a secret that the United States Government was determined to keep buried at Hyde Park, NY. They knew that the less people saw, touched, or handled the corpse, the less chance they risked of the inevitable truth leaking out.

An interesting article ran in the *New York Times* on January 4, 2010 written by Lawrence K. Altman, M.D. The article introduced a new book by Dr. Steven Lomazow and a journalist Eric Fettman entitled *F.D.R.'s Deadly Secret.* Dr. Lomazow writes of Roosevelt's illness:

> "His terminal illness came during wartime, and in an era when leaders' health and other personal matters were considered strictly private. With rare exceptions, journalists were complicit. They did not probe the obvious clues they saw as the president's appearance deteriorated. Over his last year, for instance, he lost about 30 pounds."

The evidence of Roosevelt's physical depletion was also noted in the article which began in 1944. They continue: "The authors point out that Turner Catledge, then a Washington correspondent for *The New York Times* and later its executive editor, did not report how awful Roosevelt looked during an interview at the White House in 1944, months before his nomination to an unprecedented fourth term.

Roosevelt was gaunt and glassy-eyed, Catledge wrote many years later; his jaw drooped, and he lost his train of thought. Others witnessed similar episodes; in an interview, Dr. Lomazow attributed them to a type of seizure often associated with strokes."

Everyone that saw FDR during those days in 1944 knew how awful he looked, but in every situation, there is a cause and a result. In trying to determine cause in this instance the authors make a very intriguing case. They continue:

"Roosevelt's cardiologist, Dr. Howard G. Bruenn, certified that he died of a cerebral hemorrhage from longstanding arteriosclerosis. Only in 1970 did Bruenn disclose in a medical journal article that for many years the president's blood pressure was dangerously high. Available records show that it had risen to 230/126 in 1944, from 128/82 in 1930, which would have contributed to heart failure. A reading moments before he died was 300/190."

What do these numbers mean? According to the National Heart Association, systolic blood pressure, the top number, which is the higher of the two numbers, measures the pressure in the arteries when the heart beats.

Diastolic blood pressure, the bottom number, the lower of the two numbers, measures the pressure in the arteries between heartbeats. Exactly what was the cause of such high blood pressure that took such a sudden toll of FDR's health beginning in 1944, just prior to his presidential reelection?

We already knew the result, but what was at the cause? After all President Roosevelt was only 63 years old and had enjoyed good health, despite his physical impairment, for the first 61 ½ years of his life.

He was boisterous, fiery, witty, and lovably pompous; yet by the time he attended the Conference at Yalta he was all but a walking corpse. Until the printing of this book no one saw fit to ask the proper questions and/or delve into what was being covered up.

Lomazow and Fettman continue to state the following:

> "Even then, doctors knew that chronic high blood pressure (hypertension) and arteriosclerosis were a potentially lethal combination that could cause heart disease and strokes. That became the standard and most plausible explanation for Roosevelt's stroke."

On April 13, 2011, History.com posted an article written by Jennie Cohen. The article was entitled "Memo from 1944 Warned FDR Would Likely Die in Office." She writes:

> "In July 1944, the eminent surgeon Frank Lahey wrote a confidential memo expressing his concern that President Franklin D. Roosevelt could not survive four more years in the White House. The public never learned of his assessment, and in April 1945 Roosevelt succumbed to a stroke just three months into his fourth term. Lahey's memo, which appears in full below, has just been released by the Lahey Clinic."

The article states that in the summer of 1944, while Roosevelt was campaigning to serve an unprecedented fourth term, "several doctors examined the president at the request of his personal physician, Ross T. McIntire."

Despite continued reports by the physicians to the American public claiming that the President was in good health, "Frank Lahey of Boston, wrote in a confidential memo that he had informed McIntire of his personal doubt that the president could survive another four years."

The article continues to state: "Nine months after Lahey wrote his memo, on April 12, 1945, Franklin D. Roosevelt succumbed to a stroke at age 63 while sitting for a portrait painting in Georgia." The following memo was provided by the Lahey Clinic which was founded by Dr. Lahey in Massachusetts in 1923.

Monday July 10, 1944.

I wish to record the following information regarding my opinion in relation to President Roosevelt's condition and to have them on record in the event there comes any criticism of me at a later date. I want to do this after having seen him in consultation, as a private record.

On Saturday, July 8, I talked with Admiral McIntire in my capacity as one of the group of three, Admiral McIntire, Dr. James Paullin of Atlanta, Georgia, and myself, who saw President Roosevelt in consultation and who have been over his physical examination, xrays and laboratory findings concerning his physical condition. I have reviewed all of his xrays and findings over the past years and compared them with the present findings and am recording my opinion concerning Mr. Roosevelt's condition and capacities now. I am recording these opinions in the light of having informed Admiral McIntire Saturday afternoon July 8, 1944 that I did not believe that, if Mr. Roosevelt were elected President again, he had the physical capacity to complete a term. I told him that, as a result of activities in his trip to Russia he had been in a state which was, if not in heart failure, at least on the verge of it, that this was the result of high blood pressure he has now had for a long time, plus a question of a coronary damage. With this in mind it was my opinion that over the four years of another term with its burdens, he would again have heart failure and be unable to complete it. Admiral McIntire was in agreement with this.

In addition to that I stated that it was not my duty to advise concerning whether or not such a term was undertaken, but to inform Admiral McIntire, as his family physician my opinion concerning his capacity to do it and that it was my opinion that it was Admiral McIntire's duty to inform him concerning his capacity.

In addition to the above I have told Admiral McIntire that I feel strongly that if he does accept another term, he had a very serious responsibility concerning who is the Vice President. Admiral McIntire agrees with this and has, he states, so informed Mr. Roosevelt.

I am putting this on record, I am asking that it be witnessed, sealed and placed in safe keeping. It is to be opened and utilized only in the event that there might be criticism of me should this later eventuate and the criticism be directed toward me for not having made this public. As I see my duty as a physician, I cannot violate my professional position nor possible professional confidence, but I do wish to be on record concerning possible later criticism.

[signature]

WITNESS
[signature] L. M. Straud

It should appear obvious at this point that there was a great effort made by the United States Government, specifically Roosevelt's cardiologist Dr. Howard G. Bruenn, Roosevelt's personal physician Admiral Ross T. McIntire, Dr James Paullin, surgeon Frank Lahey and his witness to the above letter, L.M. Straud, to conceal President Roosevelt's failing health prior to his bid for re-election in 1944. Shouldn't the voters have been informed prior to FDR's re-election bid of his worsening physical and mental capability not only to serve as the leader of the American people, but to serve as a representative at the Yalta Conference, where the post-war world was decided and the forming of the UN was established?

In withholding this information from the world, information which could have easily jeopardized multiple millions of lives as well as the future security of all of mankind, these doctors willingly and knowingly put at risk generations of human beings. Why?

Let your mind puzzle on that for a moment while I remind everyone of the legal definition of conspiracy. According to the Cornell University Law School, the definition of conspiracy is: *"an agreement between two or more people to commit an illegal act, along with the intent to achieve the agreement's goal."*

So before we go any further we can already establish the fact that there was a conspiracy by members of the United States Government regarding President Roosevelt's health and cause of death. We aren't even halfway through this chapter, and already we have a proven conspiracy against the American people.

It is an interesting side note that the theft of President Roosevelt's medical records happened at the United States Naval Hospital in Bethesda, Maryland. This is the same place where President John F. Kennedy's autopsy photo manipulations, autopsy report embellishments and phony entry and exit wounds were artificially carved into his body immediately after it arrived there from Dallas. In fact, after interviewing witnesses that had participated both in the Bethesda autopsy of JFK's body and the preparing and transporting of JFK's body when it left Parkland Memorial Hospital in Dallas, it was found that none of the descriptions matched at all! Literally nothing aligned.

The description of the corpse, the clothing, the head wrapping, the exit and entry wounds and even the type and color of the casket that the body had been placed in were completely and totally different.

Something very odd and very sinister happened to President Kennedy's corpse on that 1336 mile journal taken by Air Force One. In 1963 we thought that the funny business that happened at Bethesda was a once in a lifetime occurrence.

It is now looking quite clear that the JFK cover-up was just another in the line of governmental lies manufactured there as the funny business involving the Roosevelt cover-up now reveals. The big question is why? If this was a natural death of a 63 year-old President that was nothing more or nothing less than a man suffering from hypertension resulting in a fatal stroke, why the cover up?

Why, in Dr. Lahey's letter, which had been concealed for 66 years, was he trying so desperately to distance himself and shed whatever blame might come from a future discovery onto Roosevelt's personal physician Admiral McIntire?

Stop reading for ten seconds and answer these two questions: why lock the medical records up in the first place, and why make them vanish? The only logical answers to these questions are as follows: there was some variety of forbidden knowledge in the medical records that was worthy of locking them away from public view, and that same knowledge was obviously worthy of their permanent disappearance.

To add to the already glaring conspiracy against the American people I submit the following: the facts established by three doctors of President Roosevelt's condition are indisputable. FDR's development of heart failure, high blood pressure and coronary damage beginning in 1943 are both factual and well-documented, but what was the cause behind their timing and their origin? This is the logical place for further digging to begin.

After an investigation into the facts, FDR's deteriorating heath began immediately after he returned from the Tehran Conference which was hosted between November 28th and December 1st of 1943. Below is a photo of the three leaders during their meeting in Tehran. Look at the President Roosevelt's condition.

He shows all the indications of a healthy man with a full mental and physical capacity. Look closely and pay particular attention to the expression, color contrast and fullness of Roosevelt's face.

Exactly seven months and nine days after this photograph of a healthy President, Dr. Lahey wrote his now famous memo of July 10, 1944, stating that FDR was in such poor health that he wouldn't survive another term.

Compare the prior image with the photo of the Yalta Conference from February 4th to 11th of 1945. Look at the President's condition. The depletion of both his physical and mental capacity is obvious. The expression, color contrast and sunken nature of Roosevelt's face tell the whole story.

It appears obvious that Dr. Lahey's determination of the President's health was correct, but the real question is why? What happened in those seven short months to make the President's mental and physical capacity deteriorate?

Interestingly enough, FDR wasn't the only American dignitary feeling the ill effects between the Tehran and Yalta conferences. After an unexplained illness that had lasted several months, one of FDR's closest friends and most trusted military advisors, Major General Edwin Watson, died of a cerebral hemorrhage on February 20th.

The 61-year-old senior military aide and personal secretary to the President died at sea aboard the destroyer, U.S.S. Quincy, during the 8,052-mile journey back to Washington DC.

Watson carried out his duty to his country, attending the Yalta Conference where the three leaders negotiated the future of Europe. According to page 36 of William Hassett's book, *Off The Record With FDR*, Watson was also appointed the President's secretary, handling his daily appointments beginning in 1938 after the illness of Roosevelt's previous secretary, Marvin H. McIntyre.

Ironically, McIntyre also died of a cerebral hemorrhage in 1943. Watson was a key figure in Roosevelt's cabinet and was present at the most pivotal moments of WWII including both the Tehran and Yalta conferences and the development of the Atlantic Charter.

He was, in all respects, FDR's right-hand man, and was also in constant contact with America's field generals, including, but not limited to Douglas MacArthur and Admiral Nimitz.

By the time Roosevelt and Watson had returned from the Yalta conference, both men were dead. FDR just didn't know it yet. Oddly, there would be no autopsy or embalmment for Watson, either.

President Roosevelt, hit particularly hard by the loss of his closest friend, attended Watson's funeral on February 28th, while in such poor health that he never left his car to join the Joint Chiefs of Staff who participated in the full military honors at the ceremony.

Watson's death was so strange that, within a handful of years after President Roosevelt's death, author Emanuel Josephson wrote the book *The Strange Death of Franklin D. Roosevelt.* The book speculates about both Watson's and Roosevelt's deaths, and has remained one of the most persistent presidential conspiracy theories in the nation's history, a theory long preceding the magnificent works of authors Mark Lane, Don Adams, Robert Groden and Dr. Cyril Wecht regarding the JFK assassination.

FDR, having been informed by numerous doctors in July of 1944 that he was a dying man, refused to surrender his ego and step down from his post. The arrogance of a dying man who insisted on running for yet another presidential election, his fourth term, is unconscionable. This was common among egomaniacs and dictators, such as his Communist mentor Woodrow Wilson.

In 1919, during his second term, President Wilson suffered a stroke leaving him partially paralyzed, partially blind, and emotionally reckless. As it would with FDR, history would eventually reveal Wilson's physical deterioration, but only after his death in 1923. Woodrow Wilson and Franklin Roosevelt both modeled themselves and their power after the Communist Dictators of Europe and neither were willing to give up their control. If they had surrendered both their egos and their pride, they may have been able to extend their lives.

Nonetheless, the odds of having FDR, his closest advisor Major General Edwin Watson, and his correspondence secretary Marvin H. McIntyre, all dying of a cerebral hemorrhage between those years would be unfathomable.

It should appear obvious at this point that there was an outside force at play creating these symptoms and mysterious deaths. Killings on the battlefield are expected by the population and well-documented in the history books, but the war that no one sees is in military intelligence. A beehive of activity surrounded the top brass of every nation to safeguard the decision makers and keep them safe from harm.

Leaders, their generals, and their top officers are never safe when nations go to war, and British Prime Minister Winston Churchill was no exception. Churchill had survived dozens of assassination attempts thanks to Britain's secret service equivalent, MI5, along with a healthy dose of luck.

Quite possibly the most bizarre and outlandish assassination attempt on Churchill's life came in 1943. Four Nazi assassins with orders to kill him on his return flight from North Africa had cracked the British code and had established a downright goofy assassination plan. In a scene right out of an Austin Powers movie Churchill nearly got his head blown off his shoulders by an exploding chocolate bar. The complete story was featured in *The Daily Mail* on July 17, 2012, and written by Nick Enoch. Mr. Enoch writes the following:

> "Secret wartime papers exchanged between MI5 officials reveal that the Nazis' plans to conquer Britain included a deadly assault on Sir Winston Churchill with exploding chocolate. Adolf Hitler's bomb-makers coated explosive devices with a thin layer of rich dark chocolate, then packaged it in expensive-looking black and gold paper. The Germans planned to use secret agents working in Britain to discreetly place the bars of chocolate - branded as Peter's Chocolate - among other luxury items taken on trays into the dining room used by the War Cabinet during the Second World War.
>
> British agents foiled the plot and tipped off one of MI5's most senior intelligence chiefs, Lord Victor Rothschild. He typed a letter to a talented illustrator seconded to his unit asking him to draw poster-size images of the chocolate to warn the public to be on the look-out for the bars."

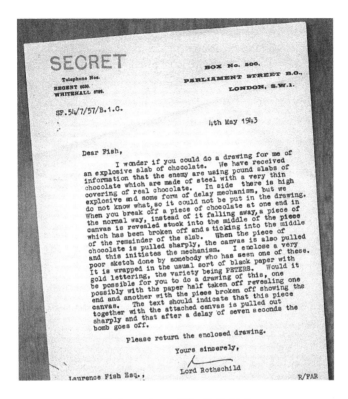

Fortunately for Winston Churchill and the Allies, the Germans' elaborate plan was foiled by a cipher school that intercepted the transmissions and was able to notify the Allied leaders. German Chancellor Adolph Hitler was extremely active in hatching assassination schemes against all of the Allied leaders.

One of his most elaborate was entitled Operation Long Jump. This plot was carefully planned, and had the full intention of assassinating Winston Churchill, President Roosevelt, and the Soviet leader Joseph Stalin during the 1943 Tehran Conference.

Just prior to the Allied meeting, German agent Otto Skorzeny and five subordinates were dropped by parachute in Iranian territory. Their plan was simple, to kill the Allied leaders, and their plan nearly worked. Unfortunately for the Fatherland, their mission was discovered by Soviet agents who captured the saboteurs.

Adolph Hitler fared no better. On the conservative side, from 1933 until 1944 there were at least 42 attempts made on Hitler's life. Everything from random people wielding guns and poisons to elaborate plans such as: the 20 July plot (aka Operation Valkyrie), Operation Spark, Oster Conspiracy and Operation Foxley. A great portion of these organized plots were sponsored by Franklin Roosevelt, Winston Churchill, and Joseph Stalin.

One such plot backfired severely and resulted in the death of Erwin Rommel. Biography.com notes the following: "After the 1944 July Plot—an assassination attempt against Hitler that occurred on July 20, 1944—Rommel's contact with the conspirators was revealed, thus implicating him in the plot to overthrow Hitler.

Rommel was then offered the option of taking his own life to avoid a public trial and protect his family. On the October 14, 1944, German officers took Erwin Rommel from his home to a remote location. There he took his own life by biting into a cyanide capsule. He was 52 years old. Rommel was given a full military burial."

The plot they speak of that occurred on July 20th, 1944 was *Operation Valkyrie.* On that date an exploding briefcase was placed with the intention of killing Adolph Hitler; it nearly found its target.

Hitler's bodyguards and their German intelligence counterparts were very good at their jobs, but there were many occasions where Hitler escaped with his life by mere luck. "Operation Valkyrie" was one of those times.

Joseph Stalin was also a target for assassination on numerous occasions, nearly all of them came at the hands of Adolph Hitler and his Nazi intelligence agents. In the mid-1930s a group of German terrorists planned to blow up Lenin's Mausoleum at a time when Stalin was physically present. This plan to kill Stalin failed. In early 1943, a soldier tried to shoot Stalin as he rode in an automobile in Red Square; the soldier was later executed.

One of the most elaborate Nazi plans to assassination Stalin was code named "Operation Zeppelin." This particular plan was designed to kill Stalin right in the middle of the Soviet capital city, Moscow.

The plan involved a secret flight by a German transport plane to a landing in the Russian countryside fifty-five miles from the Soviet capital. There, a German operative posing as a Soviet would provide a motorcycle, weapons, and proper documentation to the assassins who had been training for their mission for months.

The assassins, now well-equipped, would ride into Moscow, kill Stalin, and during the commotion hide out in a secured location. From there, with the proper citizenship paperwork, an average motorcycle ride out of the country would be easily accomplished. In the end Stalin escaped assassination as the transport plane was shot down and the assassins were caught and captured by a Soviet sentry.

Unlike President Roosevelt, Joseph Stalin managed to successfully escape assassination during the Second World War, but by the early 1950's he became so paranoid that he suspected everyone of plotting against him. His world was reduced into a circle of suspicion, isolation, and complete paranoia. He would eventually die in 1953, of, you guessed it, a cerebral hemorrhage, just like Roosevelt, Watson, and McIntyre.

Michael Wines, a *New York Times* columnist, published the following article on March 5, 2005, entitled: "New Study Supports Idea Stalin Was Poisoned." He writes:

"The authors [of the book Stalin's Last Crime] Vladimir P. Naumov, a Russian historian, and Jonathan Brent, a Yale University Soviet scholar, suggest that the most likely suspect, if Stalin was poisoned, is Beria, for 15 years his despised minister of internal security. Beria supposedly boasted of killing Stalin on May Day, two months after his death. "I did him in! I saved all of you," he was quoted as telling Vyacheslav M. Molotov, another Politburo member, in Khrushchev's 1970 memoirs, Khrushchev Remembers."

The authors indicate that according to the medical report, Stalin suffered extensive stomach hemorrhaging during his death as evidence in the twenty page official medical record, a symptom that a poison had entered his body and created not only the brain hemorrhage but stomach hemorrhaging as well.

Wines continues:

> ". . . an exhaustive study of long-secret Soviet records lends new weight to an old theory that he was actually poisoned, perhaps to avert a looming war with the United States. The 402-page book, "Stalin's Last Crime," will be published later this month. Relying on a previously secret account by doctors of Stalin's final days, its authors suggest that he may have been poisoned with Warfarin, a tasteless and colorless blood thinner also used as a rat killer, during a final dinner with four members of his Politburo."

The death drug of the day was Warfarin, with President Roosevelt, US Major General Edwin Watson, and US correspondence secretary Marvin H. McIntyre all dying of the same symptoms and description (just as Stalin had years later). All died of a stroke due to a cerebral hemorrhage.

The odds of this just "happening" that way during those years would be unfathomable. It should appear obvious at this point that there was an outside force at play creating these symptoms and mysterious deaths. Was President Roosevelt was given a fatal dose of Warfarin with his lunch, which created the "terrific headache" that he claimed he had just prior to his death? That explains FDR's death itself, but doesn't explain the rapid deterioration of his physical and mental state between the Tehran Conference in1943 and the Yalta Conference in 1945.

What was causing Roosevelt's prolonged heart failure, erratic high blood pressure, mental changes, weight loss, changes in coloring and appearance, lack of coordination and coronary damage? Warfarin was not the answer to these questions. It's obvious that something else is at work which was causing these sudden and mysterious health complications.

Consider the article previously mentioned in this chapter outlining Roosevelt's ailments written by Lawrence K. Altman M.D. in *The New York Times* on January 4, 2010:

> - Over his last year, for instance, he lost about 30 pounds.
>
> - Roosevelt was gaunt and glassy-eyed, Catledge wrote many years later; his jaw drooped, and he lost his train of thought.
>
> - Available records show that it [his blood pressure] had risen to 230/126 in 1944, from 128/82 in 1930, which would have contributed to heart failure. A reading moments before he died was 300/190.
>
> - Even then, doctors knew that chronic high blood pressure (hypertension) and arteriosclerosis were a potentially lethal combination that could cause heart disease and strokes. That became the

standard and most plausible explanation for Roosevelt's stroke.

Now ask yourself two more questions; Why is it that FDR's doctor, Admiral Ross McIntire, his cardiologist, Dr. Howard Bruenn, and specialist Dr. James Paullin felt it necessary to call in one of the most imminent doctors in the nation at the time, Dr. Frank Lahey to look ". . . over his [FDR's] physical examination, x-rays, laboratory findings concerning his physical condition."

FDR obviously did not die from the advance of polio, as four doctors would not have been necessary to determine it. My final question is possibly the best one yet. How does erratic high blood pressure, mental changes, weight loss, changes in coloring and appearance, lack of coordination and coronary damage warrant an appointment with a surgeon? Why would a prominent surgeon such as Lahey waste his precious time seeing such a patient that he knew he wouldn't be able to help?

It couldn't appear any more obvious that McIntire, Paullin, and Bruenn were completely baffled as to the cause of the president's condition. President Roosevelt seeing a surgeon at this point was the equivalent of a Hail Mary pass toward the end zone of a football game in the closing seconds. This was an act of total desperation, because they were clueless.

While the sympathetic media of the day, influenced largely by the pro-labor Democrats and their ties to the Communist infiltrated Labor Unions, were keeping President Roosevelt's true condition away from the American people, everyone else, including people in other nations, knew the truth.

Just as the Communists had infiltrated the Democrat Party, enemy spies had infiltrated the White House. To prove just how accessible the Roosevelt White House was to spying, a report of FDR's health came to Berlin from Hitler's secret service spy Admiral Wilhelm Canaris.

The message, which was leaked from sources inside the White House in mid–1941, was relayed by an airliner to a Chinese territory controlled by the Japanese. From there the message made its way through Shanghai, and with the help of the Japanese government, to its final destination in Berlin. According to the book *FDR's Deadly Secret:*

> "It was one of a series of regular updates on Roosevelt's health relayed by Count Friedrich Sauerma, an *Abwehr* agent code-named Dinter, who claimed to have a direct pipeline to the president's doctors and who picked up his information on the D.C. society circuit-of which Stirling and his family were a leading part."

On page 86 in their book they reveal the contents of the transmission:

> "Reliable source confirms that Roosevelt is suffering from uremic condition causing serious disturbances of consciousness as a result of

constant application of catheter in urinary tract. Recurrent announcements indicating mild soreness of throat and similar illnesses are merely to camouflage his true condition."

In Berlin, Nazi medical experts reading Sauerma's dispatch wrote ominously of "the morbid condition of the President's blood caused by his inability to excrete urinary matter."

The fact that the Nazi medical experts were arriving at their conclusion through third party sources which led them to miss their diagnosis is one thing, but the very idea that the enemy had a pipeline to not only the White House but Roosevelt's personal health symptoms is another.

It's extremely troubling to learn that enemy spies had so compromised our nation's security and military intel that they may have even had a connection to FDR's doctor as well. Let your mind feast on that for the moment while you ask yourself another question, could one of those people have murdered President Roosevelt?

4
The Suspects

"Death is the solution to all problems – no man, no problem."

- Joseph Stalin -

The answer to the question raised at the end of the previous chapter is a resounding yes, but exactly who could get close enough to harm FDR and how could they do it? It's time to separate the fact from the fiction and find the person responsible for the deed.

That is the sole purpose of this chapter, and I will do it in the same fashion that criminal investigators have been generating suspects for decades. When a crime is investigated, facts are gathered in an attempt to find those responsible so they can be brought before the courts and the law-and-order process can determine either their innocence or guilt.

That's how the American criminal justice system functions—at least in theory. In discussing this process with the attorneys mentioned in the acknowledgment of this book, I have learned that this is an art form that's been carefully examined and steadily improved for centuries.

When the facts are examined, criminal investigators put their personal feelings aside and follow the flow of the evidence to individuals called *persons of interest*. A *person of interest* is a phrase used by law enforcement to accompany the name of a person

113

involved in their investigation but who has not been formally accused or charged with a crime. The term has no true legal meaning but sounds very flashy for the media and lets the public know that something is being done. In reality, a person of interest could be a witness, bystander or someone with whom law enforcement speaks for the purpose of conducting the official investigation.

From there, detectives can screen and sift through witnesses and other persons of interest to find their suspects, and eventually make their arrests. This isn't an easy process or a process based on speed—it's a process based on the methodical gathering and examination of persons, facts and the *Due Process of Law.*

This exacting process outlines three elements in the process of finding a suspect. The three elements are motive, means and opportunity. Each suspect must have, within the findings of the crime, the motive, means, and opportunity to achieve the given result.

This three-element theory has proven so successful that it's now the primary foundation of crime-solving. According to a popular online dictionary website the definition for each of these terms are as follows:

Motive: something (as a need or desire) that causes a person to act.

Means: the medium, method or instrument used to obtain a result.

Opportunity: a favorable juncture of circumstances causing an action.

Alternatively, Wikipedia produces the following explanation: "Respectively, they refer to: the ability of the defendant to commit the crime (means), the reason the defendant had to commit the crime (motive), and whether or not the defendant had the chance to commit the crime (opportunity).

In the obvious murder of President Franklin Roosevelt there were numerous persons of interest who should have been questioned, probed, and have had their actions explored if indeed an official investigation into this suspicious death had transpired before both the body and the case had gone cold.

Certainly everyone close to FDR should have been questioned, including the women with whom he was having extramarital affairs, the people in his cabinet, his political enemies both at home and abroad during the elections and the war, other world leaders who were supposedly allies with our country, and any one of the Communist and Nazi spies that were caught within arm's reach of him during the time period (and there were many).

President Roosevelt and his wife had established rich and personal friendships with hundreds of highly influential and deeply connected political contacts during their 12 years in the White House, yet none of them could authorize an autopsy?, a coroner's inquest?, a proper celebration befitting a famed president?, or even an open casket viewing?

FDR was buried less than 69 hours after his heart stopped, and shortly afterward his medical records were reported stolen from a safe at Bethesda Naval Hospital. This just doesn't "happen" and people don't cover things up unless there is something worthy of it.

Yet, without a single fingerprint being lifted or without one question being asked, the case of the most popular United States President of the early twentieth century was freakishly and hastily closed forever.

This not only seemed impossible, but it also borders on illegal as FDR's medical team and the coroner acted in concert to do so. In any court in the nation the previous legal definition is a conspiracy, but before we go into any wild flights of fancy we must ask who was behind it? What was their motive? To answer these questions we must first ask many others.

To begin we must delve into this information and solve the first of the three elements of a crime: Motive. We will deal with means and opportunity later on in the chapter. Admittedly, there were numerous people who were close to FDR who had an "axe to grind."

After all, people just don't kill other people without a motive, so the logical place to start would be to assemble a list of the persons of interest. Keep in mind: motive is the trickiest of the three necessary crime elements. Some potential motives are generated by fury, other potential motives are rooted in simple disappointments that eventually dissolve within a person and become lost over time.

Knowing this, it's important that we analyze each suspect closely to determine the root, and intensity behind his or her motivation. Below are persons of interest who had varied reasons to be motivated to murder. Let the investigation begin.

1. The thirty-three members of the Duquesne Spy Ring.

> Fritz Duquesne
>
> Paul Bante
>
> Max Blank
>
> Alfred E. Brokhoff
>
> Heinrich Clausing
>
> Conradin Otto Dold
>
> Rudolf Ebeling
>
> Richard Eichenlaub
>
> Heinrich Carl Eilers
>
> Paul Fehse
>
> Edmund Carl Heine
>
> Felix Jahnke
>
> Gustav Wilhelm Kaercher
>
> Josef Klein
>
> Hartwig Richard Kleiss
>
> Herman W. Lang
>
> Evelyn Clayton Lewis

Rene Emanuel Mezenen

Carl Reuper

Everett Minster Roeder

Paul Alfred W. Scholz

George Gottlob Schuh

Erwin Wilhelm Siegler

Oscar Richard Stabler

Heinrich Stade

Lilly Barbara Carola Stein

Franz Joseph Stigler

Erich Strunck

Leo Waalen

Adolf Walischewski

Else Weustenfeld

Axel Wheeler-Hill

Bertram Zenzinger

2. The eight members of Operation Pastorius.

Ernst Burger

Herbert Haupt

George John Dasch

Edward John Kerling

Richard Quirin

Heinrich Harm Heinck

Hermann Otto Neubauer

Werner Thiel

3. Lona Cohen (AKA: Helen Kroger)

4. Morris Cohen (AKA: Peter Kroger)

5. Eleanor Roosevelt

6. Marguerite 'Missy' LeHand

7. Lucy Mercer

8. Harry Hopkins

9. Elizabeth Shoumatoff

10. Nicholas Robbins

11. Arthur Prettyman

12. Henrietta Nesbitt

13. Howell Crim

14. Winston Churchill

I. MOTIVE

Motive: something (as a need or desire) that causes a person to act

1. The 33 members of the Duquesne Spy Ring.

The Duquesne Spy Ring, the largest convicted espionage network in American history, was launched by Nazi Germany with the intention of gathering military information, carrying out acts of sabotage and the assassination of key personnel. Did one of these people murder FDR to fulfill their duty to the Fatherland?

2. The eight members of Operation Pastorius.

Operation Pastorius was another German spy ring that materialized on American soil immediately following the Japanese attack on Pearl Harbor. The eight members of the spy ring were commanded by Hitler to sabotage the American war effort by focusing on attacking civilian targets, as well as American heads of state and other high-ranking officials. Was one of their bullseyes on the highest head of state in the USA?

3. Eleanor Roosevelt

I know it may seem ridiculous to put this famous woman in this investigation, but famous people murder too. For this investigation we must forget who this person was and focus on the investigation itself. As the wife of President Roosevelt, she was the nation's First Lady for nearly four terms in office. She was also FDR's cousin who despised Franklin's controlling mother and his romantic affair with Lucy Mercer.

When FDR's romance was discovered she offered him a divorce, but in order to keep up their political image, FDR refused. For the remainder of their lives the couple stayed together in a loveless marriage of convenience. Best known for her outspokenness on racial and women's rights issues, she hated Lucy Mercer and forbade FDR from seeing her again. Lucy was, however, romantically involved with FDR the week prior to his sudden death and was present at the time of his death. Eleanor, however, was not. Was Eleanor Roosevelt a jilted lover? Was she so tired of FDR's infidelity that she arranged FDR's murder? Or, did she murder FDR herself?

4. Marguerite 'Missy' LeHand

Missy LeHand had come to work as Franklin's secretary. Over the years, they developed a very close relationship, with Missy serving as one of Franklin's main friends and confidantes. She lived in the White House during his presidency, and when she suffered a stroke, Franklin altered his will to include her.

Eleanor and all the children were warm towards Missy and considered her one of the family. Franklin's son, Elliott, later revealed that his father and Missy had a long affair, and it seems likely that the family was aware. Was Missy LeHand a jilted lover? Was she so madly in love with FDR that she would have rather killed him than shared him? Did her blood boil when she learned of FDR's affair with Lucy Mercer?

5. Lucy Mercer

Mercer took a position as the social secretary of Eleanor Roosevelt and started a romantic affair with FDR in 1916. The romance was discovered by Eleanor when she found their love letters. Although she wanted a divorce, political and familial pressures caused them to remain in the hollow marriage. Franklin told his wife that he had terminated the affair and promised his wife that he wouldn't see Mercer again. The truth of the matter was far different than the promise as Lucy and Franklin maintained a very secret and very close relationship for almost thirty years. Was Lucy Mercer a jilted lover? Was she so madly in love with FDR that she would have rather killed him than shared him?

6. Harry Hopkins

Hopkins was one of FDR's closest advisers. He was so instrumental in crafting social programs of the New Deal that he was often referred to as a co-president in certain inner circles. In World War II, he was FDR's top diplomatic adviser and his high-level troubleshooter. He crafted the Lend-Lease program with the Allies and had the ultimate backstage pass with all the keys to the back doors of the US government. He was specifically used in dealings with the Soviet Union and met with their high-ranking officials.

Hopkins personally explained FDR's plans to Stalin directly, and in return he lobbied the Soviets' point of view as well. He was far kinder to the Soviets than others thought he should have been in adding them to the Lend-Lease Program. With FDR being handicapped and having limited mobility, Hopkins ran almost everything. He was the most important man that no one ever knew; he was also discovered decades later to have been a Soviet spy and operative. In warfare no leader is ever safe, and those with access like Hopkins could kill under orders at random.

7. Elizabeth Shoumatoff

Shoumatoff was a Russian-born artist who immigrated to the United States during the Russian Revolution. Settling in Locust Valley, New York, in the mid-1930s, she met and befriended Lucy Mercer. A remarkably talented and self-taught artist and watercolor painter, she was hired to paint a portrait of President Roosevelt in 1943 and again in 1945. Admittedly, she didn't like FDR. In fact, in her book, *FDR's Unfinished Portrait*, is a conversation between her and Lucy Mercer. She writes:

> "Tell me [Schoumatoff to Mercer], is he sincere?" That he lacked sincerity was upon which most of my friends were unanimous, while my own thoughts about him were inconclusive. Her answer was most affirmative, but it still did not convince me. She continued about talking about Roosevelt in admiring terms. So many qualities were brought up that I do not remember them all. We discussed his extraordinary ability to work, his dynamic approach to anything he undertook, and his greatness in general. This conversation did not develop any further because, in all honesty, I could not join in her enthusiasm."

The anti-Roosevelt comments from her clients written in her book are too numerous to add, but the Du Pont family (chemicals and paints), George Eastman (Kodak film), Harvey Firestone (tires), Samuel Colgate (toothpaste), Henry Ford (automobile), the Frick family (of Carnegie steel fame), the Heinz family (catsup), James Hilton (hotels), the Mellon family (world banks),

William Tubman (President of Liberia), and Robert Woodruff (chairmen of the board of Coca-Cola) were not fans of FDR. His New Deal and anti-business legislation were costing these people a small fortune. They would have paid any amount of money to rid the economy of him, and now, finally, they knew of someone who had open and free access to him.

There are other telling morsels quoted in her book about the people around her hating FDR. On page 91 of her book Elizabeth says the following about her brother: "For years my brother had been anything but an admirer of Roosevelt. . ." Aside from her brother, her book is peppered with comments from her entire client list of high-profile businessmen whose disdain for Roosevelt and his anti-business policies couldn't have been overstated.

The Russian artist was at Warm Springs, Georgia, when Roosevelt died. Was Shoumatoff a Soviet spy and assassin? Was her dislike for FDR so great that she was paid by her high-profile client list to murder him?

8. Nicholas Robbins

Robbins was a longtime friend of Shoumatoff. He was also Russian born and was a photographer by trade. He was the driver of the car that brought Elizabeth Shoumatoff to Warm Springs, Georgia. His photos of her portrait subjects helped Shoumatoff with her paintings. Like Shoumatoff, he was in close contact with an entire host of anti-FDR elite, to say nothing of his Soviet background and contacts. Was being present on the day that Roosevelt died with another Russian at his side a mere coincidence? Was the Russian Robbins, like Shoumatoff, a paid assassin? Were they working together?

9. Arthur Prettyman

Prettyman was one of FDR's personal valets and was on duty with the president at the time of his death in Warm Springs Georgia. Prettyman was one of many valets that FDR had throughout his presidency. Because of his physical handicap, FDR relied on his personal valets for everything including lifting, dressing, bathing and other varieties of personal grooming. They were always close by. Did Prettyman slip something in the president's food causing the lethal result?

10. Henrietta Nesbitt

According to the White House Historical Association, the White House was led by "housekeeper Henrietta Nesbitt and a succession of chief ushers." Mrs. Nesbitt was "a Hyde Park neighbor of the Roosevelts who had worked with ER [Eleanor Roosevelt] in the local Hyde Park League of Women Voters chapter, had little experience beyond running a home bakery when she accepted the job. ER, despite family complaints about meal planning, found Nesbitt 'a lifesaver'." Nesbitt was very close to Mrs. Roosevelt, and when word of FDR's affairs leaked back to her, she was furious at what the president was putting Eleanor through. Was her friendship with the scorned Mrs. Roosevelt motive to poison the president?

11. Howell Crim

Crim was named Chief Usher in 1938 and oversaw the operation of the White House and its staff. His position put him in daily contact with the president and First Family on a very personal and intimate level. He was charged with the supervising the social affairs, gatherings, receptions and housings of heads of state, heads of government, diplomats, as well as other guests.

Substantial portions of his past were missing as he left the United States to travel and work abroad. Was he part of the Communist spy ring that already existed within the White House? Was he part of the *Silverman Group* of Communists within FDR's administration as the defecting Soviet spy, Elizabeth Bentley, claimed?

12. Winston Churchill

FDR and Churchill didn't always see eye to eye. In fact there was at least one documented instance in 1943 where the two men sparred over Roosevelt's intention to dismantle most of the British colonies, which were located all across the world from Britain's four centuries of conquest, and to let them become their own self-governing nations. Churchill knew that England wasn't as powerful as the other two Allied nations, but he also knew that the British Empire had a strength that the others didn't.

They had the ability to launch an invasion from any number of their colonies, and that was not something Churchill was going to let FDR take from them.

Churchill had no interest in the American President imposing his will on what the English did with their property.Another point of angst between the two men included the fact that FDR was giving Stalin anything that he wanted while England, which was fighting ferocious battles to save their island, received basically nothing at the end of the war.

FDR constantly treated the sacrifice and might that the English made to the war effort as almost invisible in comparison to how he bent to Stalin's will. It wasn't long before Churchill realized that he was being treated as a second-class citizen.

The last bone of contention between them had, again, to do with Stalin. Churchill never warmed to Stalin and he knew that he wasn't going to play nice in the sandbox with the other world leaders after the treaties were signed.

He predicted that Stalin would violate the terms that were set forth in the conferences and had the vision to know that this would be a major issue to the future of world peace. Roosevelt disagreed, and took Stalin at his word.

Churchill proposed a plan to mobilize the armies of the U.K. and the U.S. against the Red Army. Churchill called it *Operation Unthinkable*. The two men sparred over what would have been the July 1, 1945 attack on the Soviet Army, which Churchill deemed as the necessary start of World War III.

Churchill argued that they needed to take Stalin out before he could get any stronger. President Roosevelt hotly debated this idea with Churchill for months, even managing to convince English Generals to oppose Churchill on the matter. Eventually FDR was successful in convincing the British Chiefs of Staff Committee not to consider it. Churchill was humiliated.

SUMMARY OF MOTIVES

Each person of interest had a clear-cut motive to murder with the exception of Arthur Prettyman and Lucy Mercer. Prettyman was a close personal friend of FDR's and was haunted by the death of the president until the day of his own death, years later. In fact, Prettyman's wife claimed that the president's death impacted Arthur so deeply that he was never emotionally the same.

Although Prettyman clearly had the opportunity and access to the means to murder the president, there was simply no motive. He was, in all aspects, a loyal servant with no other connections. He was employed to take care of the president's needs and showed no interests beyond that.

Like Prettyman, Lucy Mercer was also loyal to the last. Her relationship with FDR began in secrecy and she was already aware of his extramarital dalliances. There were no surprises for Mercer and no motive to murder either. In this investigation round we can remove both Prettyman and Mercer.

The remaining persons of interest all had motives or were directly connected to greater powers that wished to murder President Roosevelt. Unlike the investigation in my first book *Who Murdered Elvis?* this murderer would not necessarily kill for personal gain. As we move into the next round of the investigation, means, the field will tighten, as not every suspect would have the access required to commit murder.

II. Means

Means: the medium, method, or instrument used to obtain a result.

1. The thirty-three members of the Duquesne Spy Ring.

All 33 of the agents in this spy ring had either plead guilty or were brought to trial and found guilty on December 13th, 1941. They were all sentenced to lengthy prison terms in Federal District Court in New York City on January 2nd, 1942. With all 33 members of the spy ring having been in custody since 1942, there would be no possible way any of the members would have had the means or the opportunity to murder President Roosevelt.

2. The eight members of Operation Pastorius.

The trial for the eight members of Operation Pastorius ended on August 3rd 1942. All were found guilty. Six were sentenced to death and were executed on August 8th, 1942 and sentenced to death. One was sentenced to life in prison and the other's sentence was shortened to thirty years. The shortened sentencing of the last two was due to the help and information they provided regarding the other members. They also turned themselves in, which garnered special leniency from FDR who intervened to alter their sentencing. The other members were executed on the August 8th, 1942 in the electric chair. With the members either executed or in custody a full three years prior to the President's death, none of them would have had the means or the opportunity to murder President Roosevelt.

3. Eleanor Roosevelt

Did the first lady have the means to murder the president? Let's ponder this for a moment. She obviously had full run of the White House and had close personal contacts with the staff. She also had ample contact to multiple members within the government who were both friendly and unfriendly to FDR. Knowing the German and Soviet spy rings that existed both in and around the White House during the time period, it would have been altogether possible that she not only had the means herself, but with very little effort could have come in contact with the means to murder.

4. Marguerite 'Missy' LeHand

Did Missy LeHand have the means to murder the president? Missy lived in the White House during FDR's term in office, and because she was added to his will after he was stricken with illness she certainly had ample motive to kill. Did she have the means? Because she lived on site and was in close proximity to FDR as well as the rest of the White House employees, she not only had the means herself, but with very little effort could have come in contact with the means to murder.

5. Harry Hopkins

Beyond question, Hopkins had the means to murder FDR. Through his various and continued contact with his Soviet and Marxist counterparts in Stalin's regime, Hopkins could have murdered FDR at any hour of any day and in multiple ways. With his backstage pass to the Soviet and the American governments, the murder could have been done with great ease and covered up immediately.

6. Elizabeth Shoumatoff

Did Elizabeth Shoumatoff have the means to murder the president? Without question she did. Not only did she have access to a myriad of elite businessmen through her client list who would have supplied her with anything from poison to swords to commit the murder, she wasn't fond of him herself.

America's business elite couldn't vote his profit-squashing programs out of office, so killing him may have been their only option. They would have been all too eager to use her as an assassin and would have supplied her with the means.

7. Nicholas Robbins

Like Elizabeth Shoumatoff, his contact with her client elite within the business world would have been given him the means to murder the president.

8. Henrietta Nesbitt

Mrs. Nesbitt had access to the whole of the White house and could have offered her free-flowing backstage pass to any number of FDR's enemies in order to do a countless number of ill-fated deeds.

9. Howell Crim

His position at the White House put him in daily contact with the President and First Family as he supervised social affairs, gatherings, receptions and the housings of heads of state, and diplomats, as well as other guests. Crim is another person of the inner circle that couldn't swing a dead cat without hitting a Roosevelt. He also worked closely with Mrs. Nesbitt to ensure that the food served was perfectly aligned with FDR's wishes to receive his many visitors.

10. Winston Churchill

With the English not seen as a threat to anyone in America during the war years, there was always a handful of Churchill's loyalists within arm's reach of the President, if not Churchill himself, who visited the Oval Office regularly. Could he have given orders to an associate in the states to murder FDR?

Like the First Lady and Harry Hopkins; Henrietta Nesbitt, Winston Churchill, and Howell Crim all had the access to the means to murder FDR at will and the pull within the White House to do so. Any one of them could have come into contact with the various spy rings in and around the White House that were later revealed after FDR's death.

SUMMARY OF MEANS

As expected, the list narrows as we filter each *person of interest* through the second phase of the process to determine who had the ability to commit the crime and the medium, method, or instrument used to obtain a result. Excluded from the investigation at this level are the Duquesne Spy Ring and Operation Patorius, leaving Eleanor Roosevelt, Missy Lehand, Elizabeth Shoumatoff, Nicholas Robbins, Henrietta Nesbitt and Howell Crim to enter the third and last phase of the investigation, which is opportunity. As we continue the investigation, the field will again narrow to reveal the prime suspects in the case.

III. Opportunity

Opportunity: a favorable juncture of circumstances causing an action

1. Eleanor Roosevelt

With ample knowledge of FDR's extramarital affairs and free access to the whole of the White House, as well as all the political friends and enemies in Washington D.C., she obviously had the motive and the means to murder the president, however she only had the rare opportunity to do so. She was very busy being a champion of her many humanitarian causes and was rarely in the same place as FDR. This shocked me while I was doing the many hours of research.

Apparently the First Lady and FDR only saw each other face to face a handful of times a month, and after his affairs were discovered were more or less passersby. Naturally they maintained appearances for the cameras, but things between them were lukewarm at best. Simply put, Eleanor Roosevelt had no interest in being anywhere around FDR when he died, but used her status as the First Lady to further her independence and recognition. Although limited, she did have the opportunity to murder.

2. Marguerite 'Missy' LeHand

Like the First Lady, LeHand had ample and free access to the White House, its staff, its political cronies on both sides (those who loved and hated the president), as well as all the Soviet and Nazi spies in and around Washington at the time (which were not revealed until decades later).

3. Harry Hopkins

Although not present when FDR died, he had the opportunity, through collusion, to murder. Like Mercer, he has also cleared both motive and means. Hopkins has now joined the ranks of the murder suspects.

4. Elizabeth Shoumatoff

Shoumatoff, like the previous two, was also present and in direct contact with President Roosevelt when he died. She had already passed the motive and the means elements and now has passed the opportunity element as well. Clearing all three takes her from a mere person of interest and converts her into a murder suspect.

5. Nicholas Robbins

As Robbins was under the employ of Shoumatoff for the week that they were working on Roosevelt's portrait, and he was assisting her by taking photography stills, he obviously had ample access to the President. Like the artist herself, Robbins has now been transformed into a murder suspect.

6. Henrietta Nesbitt

Mrs. Nesbitt was far more loyal to the First Lady and she was not at all pleased with FDR's conquests of the flesh outside of his marriage, which seems to have been common knowledge and widely known. Mrs. Nesbitt had the opportunity to murder as she had daily access to the President.

7. Howell Crim

Like the Nesbitt, Crim was not in the proximity of Warm Springs, Georgia, when the President was murdered, as he was busy coordinating the functions and affairs at the White House in Washington D.C. However, he did have free and equal access to the president and had the opportunity to murder. Like Mrs. Nesbitt, Howell Crim shared a backstage pass to anything that might have gone on at the White House.

8. Winston Churchill

The vast spy network of the oldest and most established country in the trio of Allied nations indeed had a long reach. Churchill could have probably instructed someone to reach out and touch anything in the White House that he wanted, but not in Warm Springs, Georgia. To my knowledge and to the vast extent of research that I have done on the subject, Churchill wasn't connected in any way to the people there except for the possibility of a casual acquaintance. Churchill will be dropped at this point in the investigation.

SUMMARY OF OPPORTUNITY

At this stage of the investigation the field has seven persons of interest. They are Eleanor Roosevelt, Harry Hopkins, Elizabeth Shoumatoff, Nicholas Robbins, Henrietta Nesbitt, Howell Crim and Missy LeHand. Dropped from the list is Winston Churchill. Each of the people had the motive, means and opportunity to murder the president. Turning these people into full blown murder suspects has nothing to do with my personal opinion of these people, and everything to do with the situation that left the 32nd President of the United States of America dead on April 12, 1945. As an investigator of the situation I am merely following where the facts of the matter lead me, and in doing so, it is now becoming clear that one of these people, or a combination of these people, murdered President Roosevelt.

EXAMINING THE SUSPECTS

All good investigators have one thing in common: They ignore their personal likes and dislikes and follow the evidence connecting the dots to solve the crime. In the seventy plus years since FDR's murder, this has been a major stumbling block as no one, until myself, has had the balls to add people like the First Lady to the list of suspects.

In this venue I don't care about her prestige, her good works or her gentle nature. To me she is just another warm body to be factored. In this situation, with so many random people involved in the mix of personalities, only an outside investigator could draw the necessary conclusions and find the murderer.

Since I've never met FDR, or anyone mentioned in this book, factoring my personal likes and dislikes wasn't an issue. Other people are consumed with making friends, which is a good pastime, but I write these "Who Murdered?" books to solve murders, not make friends. Simply put: I don't care who murdered this man as long as we find the murderer.

In my first book *Who Murdered Elvis?* I was able to separate the remaining murder suspects into two groups of people who shared the common motive to proceed with the investigation. That was a lengthy process which established the connection between the people within each group, which calculated their possible modes and arrangements of the murder. Based on the research of those two groups, the murderer was found and the mode of murder was expanded and explained. This book will be no different as we divide the groups for analysis.

Group One Analysis

As we examine Group One, consisting of Elizabeth Shoumatoff, Nicholas Robbins, and Harry Hopkins, we can link them together and hypothesize how and why the murder occurred. With Shoumatoff, Robbins, and Hopkins, all roads went through Stalin.

All three were Russian loyalists, all three had been linked to Soviet spy rings in one form or the next and all three had backgrounds of being sympathizers of Stalin. Each had individual reasons for eliminating FDR as well as reasons that could be linked to a larger whole.

Was FDR poisoned by the trio? One could easily imagine a situation where Elizabeth Shoumatoff, while painting the President's portrait, took advantage of the fact that the president was distracted by signing and sorting his official papers and correspondences. How hard would it have been for the artist to slip something in FDR's food or his drink unnoticed?

In fact, this was the testament of Shoumatoff as well as everyone else in the house. The artist, upon seeing that the president was very busy signing papers for Bill Hassett, his correspondence secretary, suggested postponing the sitting. Hassett detested the presence of the artist who was having FDR sign papers, papers that would eventually end up draped on every table, chair and sofa in the house. Roosevelt refused to have the sitting re-scheduled saying that they could get started as soon as Mr. Hassett collected his drying documents. FDR called it folding his "laundry."

> In her book she writes: "To my suggestion that we postpone the sitting, the president said, "Oh no, I'll be through in a few moments and will be ready for you." He looked cheerful and full of pep. I never realized, at the time that Mr. Hassett was irritated by my presence. From what he wrote later on, he implied that I was a nuisance, that I was measuring the president's nose, which I never do, but fundamentally he was concerned that I was tiring the president with my painting. Rather reluctantly I returned to the cottage and picked up my easel, paint box and board. When I came back, Mr. Hassett was waiting for the signed papers to dry. They were all over the room, on every chair and table, his "laundry" as the president called it."

While Shoumatoff had the president distracted, poison could have easily been put in his lunch during its careful preparation. Possibly a substance could have been added to his food after it was served as Shoumatoff was telling the president to hold his face in any number of painting poses. Could Robbins, who was in the room with the president and the artist, have poisoned FDR while his artist, and fellow Communist, had him posing with his eyes elsewhere?

And where does Hopkins fit in? Hopkins, who was more loyal to Stalin than FDR, could have been the mastermind of the operation as well as the person who handled the media spin to avoid detection. Was Stalin, who was no stranger to murdering his enemies, using poisons that the United States couldn't detect in 1945? Did that information leak to Hopkins? Regardless of our opinion, two hours after the president finished his lunch he was gravely ill and in the hour that followed he was found slumped motionless in his chair and pronounced dead.

Such an event would be highly desirable to Stalin as well as the members of the Communist Party of the United States of America (CPUSA) and their many operatives and spies that had infiltrated the President's White House staff as well as his cabinet. In the decades that passed it was discovered that Stalin, through Hopkins and many other spies, knew more about what happened in FDR's White House than his generals did.

Stalin viewed Truman as a political newbie and not the negotiator that FDR was. Surely Stalin would have rather negotiated with the inexperienced and weasel-like Truman. Killing FDR would have achieved that. After all, that was Stalin's ultimate prize, to spread communism through the postwar world. Could Stalin have used these three operatives as assassins to improve his postwar land grab? The land that he took during the war, he didn't give back.

Group Two Analysis

As we examine group 2 consisting of Henrietta Nesbitt, Eleanor Roosevelt, Howell Crim, and Missy LeHand, we can link them together and hypothesize how and why the murder occurred. With all of them either working in, or living in the White House, all roads of this group went through revenge.

Nesbitt, who was a close personal friend of the First Lady, had grown tired of President Roosevelt's marital infidelity and his many obvious affairs that were shoved in Eleanor's face. The core of the infidelity was Missy LeHand and Lucy Mercer, although there were others. LeHand lived at the White House and Mercer was a continuous visitor at the Little White House in Warm Springs, Georgia where the President died.

Is it any wonder that the First Lady was mysteriously absent in Warm Springs when FDR died? Nesbitt felt that Eleanor was far too kind to be treated with such poor regard. Missy LeHand, on the other hand, wanted the president all to herself and was tired of sharing him with the First Lady and countless others. When FDR would speak of Eleanor, Missy became violently jealous and would throw things around the room and even at the President himself.

Tired of being the "other woman," it wasn't long before LeHand began to loathe FDR. Trying to bend to LeHand's wishes, the last six months of FDR's life he was rarely around the First Lady except for the occasional media event or photo-op which was designed to maintain the public appearance that the First Family was both happy and intact. Nether were true. Howell Crim is an interesting character in his own right. Crim's upbringing and education are a mystery to researchers. About the only thing that is known about his early life is that he fled the United States prior to the First World War, surfacing in the middle of the Russian Revolution on the side of the Communists. Afterwards, he joined the United States Navy and married a woman who was a member of the Communist Party of the United States of America (CPUSA).

His duties at the White House began as an usher and grew to include the supervision of the White House staff and housekeepers, coordinating social affairs and FDR's various receptions of world diplomats and government officials. His daily contact with Mrs. Nesbitt and the First Lady opened his eyes to the harsh treatment that Eleanor Roosevelt had to endure at the hands of the president.

To make matters worse, long after the other employees had left for the day, Crim would be busy at his desk where the love struck and somber LeHand found a sympathetic ear. It wasn't long before Crim's loyalties began to shift, and not in FDR's favor.

By 1945, the swaggering and seemingly oblivious Commander in Chief was surrounded by as many Soviet and Nazi spies as he was White House staff who loathed him for his mistreatment of his wife and his extramarital affairs. After all, Eleanor always involved herself in the personal lives of the White House staff and went to great lengths to make their accommodations and working conditions as tolerable as possible.

She even had the White House remodeled for the workers so that their occupations could be carried out with greater ease and comfort. Her caring nature was not at all phony. She often attended funerals of their employees' families and would even visit the workers if they were sick or ailing. Her kindness and generosity toward the staff only made FDR's marital misdeeds appear all the more appalling—and they were.

With Nesbitt, Crim, and LeHand all aligning against FDR for various reasons and with all of them having free and ample access to the rooms, social schedules, cleaning supplies, drinkware and silverware; how impossible would it have been for these people to have FDR poisoned by doing nothing more than contaminating the articles around his place setting at any number of the scheduled White House social events?

While the analyses of both groups of suspects seem plausible, there are problems with each of the scenarios. The main problem with Group One is the myopic scope of the plan. While Shoumatoff, Robbins, and Hopkins may very well have colluded to poison FDR while he was vacationing in Warm Springs, that didn't explain the steady decline of the President's health for more than two years; a decline that seemed to baffle each and every one of the President's doctors.

The main problem with the analysis of Group Two is similar. While Eleanor Roosevelt, Mrs. Nesbitt, Howell Crim, and Missy LeHand had access to the president while he was at the White House, none of them were at Warm Springs when he died.

If these four were involved in any foul play it couldn't have happened in the time period immediately prior to the president's death due to the distance and proximity between them.

Also, if they had decided to collectively poison the president, how would they have known what substance to use to accomplish the task that would also avoid detection? Remember, they were all aware of the fact that Roosevelt had a full entourage of doctors tending to his care. Surely, they would have been caught.

Since President Roosevelt's health began to show slow and visible signs of deterioration beginning with the conference in Tehran and continuing beyond the conference in Yalta, it would have been impossible for each group of murder suspects to accomplish the broad task divided in this fashion.

Exactly seven months and nine days after the conference in Tehran, Dr. Lahey penned his now famous letter to FDR's doctors basically telling him that the President was a dead man walking. Fourteen months and four days after Dr. Lahey's letter was received, FDR died of the most baffling and sporadic symptoms recorded at that time.

President Roosevelt's myriad health ailments, symptoms, and afflictions seemed to defy both treatment and logic. From day to day, and over the course of several months, his afflictions seemed to appear entirely out of nowhere and then as fast as they appeared, they would vanish.

The president would be near death for a day or maybe two and then magically rebound from that ailment, only for another to reappear which would, in turn, also eventually retreat. Doctors, surgeons and medicines had no effect as the ailments seemed to come out of nowhere.

It is needless to say at this juncture, but I must, the entire medical community in the United States of America in the year nineteen hundred and forty-five was completely baffled. This was the designed work of a mastermind with far more adept knowledge and skill than a bunch of housekeepers, jilted lovers and miscellaneous others. The time has come to separate the dance from the dancer.

5
The Rabbit Hole

"In politics, nothing happens by accident. If it happens, you can bet it was planned that way".

- Franklin Delano Roosevelt -

A few glaring questions need to be answered immediately as there seem to be gaping holes in investigational logic. What mysterious poison could have wreaked such havoc on our president's crippled body? Why wasn't it detectable? Why were all of the doctors so clueless, and how was it being administered so readily? All of these questions need to be answered in this chapter and they certainly will be.

Let's begin by answering the first of these questions. What poison could have been used by the assassins that escaped being detected? As established in chapter 3, none of FDR's regular doctors had a clue as to what was happening with the president's health. His laundry list of symptoms seemed to put the man near death and then subside, only to have other symptoms appear. Once those symptoms were treated, others would appear, and then they would vanish.

The yo-yo effect of the president's health began at the Tehran Conference and continued until his death shortly after he attended the conference in Yalta. FDR's doctors were the cream of the crop that America had to offer for the time period, and they were baffled. This is obvious for many reasons.

No matter what they did his symptoms didn't improve, and FDR's health continued to deteriorate despite the fact that more and more doctors were called in for opinions and examinations.

Another "telltale sign" that the president's circle of physicians had no clue as to his physical condition was their arrangement for FDR to see a surgeon. A surgeon? Let your mind muse on that fact for a while. If, in fact, what they were telling everyone for the past seventy-plus years were to be taken as true, and his symptoms were merely the advance of his polio affliction, what would a surgeon possibly do for the man?

Throughout this book I have been featuring many quotes from *FDR's Deadly Secret.* I have been doing this for a reason. The medical evidence in this particular book was researched and gathered by a medical doctor who was also the book's co-author.

Because a doctor was a co-author of the book it can serve as a benchmark for FDR's medical documentation. The following excerpts from this work are listed below and their documentation of Roosevelt's aliments do not match the list of symptoms associated with the advance of polio.

Pages 101-102: "His face was pallid and there was a bluish discoloration of his skin, lips, and nail beds."

Page 102: "Appeared slightly cyanotic [the bluish discoloration] … Heart enlarged, normal rhythm, no murmurs"

Page 102: "Bruenn declared, was in acute congestive heart failure, suffering from an enlarged heart, hypertension, and hypertensive heart disease."

Page 104: "Bruenn also called for a battery of medical tests, including-significantly-a prostate exam."

Page 104: "Another test he called for was an examination of Roosevelt's eye grounds-the retinal blood vessels-for signs of hypertension."

Pages 104-105: "Lahey was particularly interested in the gastrointestinal tract"-a curious request, given that the original complaint had been bronchial, the issue at hand was cardiac failure."

Pages 158-159: Secretary of State Edward Stettinius first grew concerned as he watched the president deliver his inaugural address: "He had seemed to tremble all over. It was not just his hands that shook, but his whole body as well…. It seemed to me that some kind of deterioration in the President's health had taken place between the middle of December and the inauguration."

The following list of symptoms has been established as the afflictions associated with the advance of polio.

- Continuing muscle and joint weakness
- Muscle pain that gets worse
- Becoming easily exhausted or fatigued
- Muscle wasting, also called muscle atrophy
- Trouble breathing and/or swallowing

- Sleep-related breathing problems (sleep apnea)
- Becoming cold and/or weakness in muscles

The above list of aliments was furnished by healthline.com and checked by three private doctors that I am associated with; however, I wasn't given permission to add their names to the book due to their affiliations with certain hospitals and medical clinics as they wished to remain nameless in connection with the Roosevelt name.

Each doctor that I spoke with thought, as I do, that sending anyone suffering from the advance of polio to a surgeon was absurd. The last straw of silliness came as world renowned surgeon, Dr. Frank Lahey, gave the man a series of x-rays and continued to give his opinions of these x-rays in his now famous memo to the President's regular core of doctors (posted in Chapter 3).

This is possibly the most puzzling act and the biggest question in this investigation: why is a man whose primary complaint to his physician is heart and hypertension related issues having x-rays? Heart and hypertension issues don't reveal themselves in an x-ray.

What in the hell were these doctors doing? What could Roosevelt's doctors possibly have been looking for by consulting a surgeon who is taking x-rays? These actions and countless others speak volumes to the veritable incompetence of these physicians as the record indicates that they were indeed in search of something without having any idea what it was.

One witness said of FDR's deteriorating physical condition that his hands shook so violently he could barely light or hold his cigarette. How is this a symptom of heart complications and/or hypertension? After spending days looking through medical journals, talking with physicians, studying the various poisons and contacting one of the nation's leading forensic pathologists, there is only one answer: FDR was being slowly poisoned with lead.

Sound like an outlandish claim that would be impossible to pull off? Hardly—in fact if you look at the history of U.S. presidents as well as other leaders, especially during war, you will be amazed to see that poisoning opposition leaders has been commonplace for centuries.

While the golden age of political poisoning piqued during the Italian Renaissance, history tells us that poisoning was viewed as a legitimate weapon against the powerful since 331 BC. Possibly the most notable were Rasputin and the Apostle John and they are in good company.

Poisoning was such a common form of assassination and murder that the political and the powerful needed to safeguard themselves as well as their families. They did so by having people taste their food beforehand to see if it was safe for consumption.

These tasters, officially named "food tasters", have been an accessory of the elite for centuries. In fact, every U.S. president since the 1800s has used a similar method. Although they have evolved over the years from the days of Roman Emperor Claudius, Joseph

Stalin, Napoleon Bonaparte, Mark Antony, Cleopatra, Adolph Hitler, Queen Elizabeth I, and King Henry VIII, leaders have used everything from dogs to military prisoners to test their food. The modern-day evolution of food safety for the President in the United States has evolved from mere food tasting into an entire team which is officially called the *Presidential Food Safety Team*.

Their job is to set up a security zone where the President and the First Family are free to eat without complication. They include everything from "food screeners" (people who watch the food preparation), to an entire protection process that encompasses everything food related that enters the White house.

Although this information is supposed to be kept secret, there are those who have discussed it, and probably to the displeasure of their superiors. The following quotes are from the History Channel's documentary, *America's Book of Secrets*, episode 1, "The White House."

> "To ensure the safety of the first family every aspect of their daily needs is monitored, including the food they eat and the gifts they receive. "

> "The food that goes into the White House is screened at a remote site before it ever gets to the White House itself. So a lot of precautions are taken to ensure that whatever meals or whatever food that's going to be provided at the White House is thoroughly screened. "– W. Ralph Basham, Director of The Secret Service, 2003-2006

"If food comes as a gift, unless it's from someone who is a very close friend of a family member, the Secret Service will just throw it away, and I think that even friends and family learn that they shouldn't bring food into the White House." – Ronald Kessler, Author, *Inside The White House*

U.S. presidents and other world leaders have used "food tasters" while out of their zones of protection. This precaution was employed by President Lincoln and continues to be used today. Some of the modern-day Presidents who have used food tasters are: President Reagan, President H.W. Bush, President Clinton, President George W. Bush, President Obama and President Trump.

They are not alone, however, as Turkey's President Recep Tayyip Erdogan, Vladimir Putin, Saddam Hussein, and Mustafa Kemal Ataturk have followed suit. The threat, especially during wartime, is so great that Turkey's eighth president, who died of an apparent heart attack, was poisoned from a glass of lemonade served to him at a Bulgarian Embassy reception.

Why is it that all of these presidents and powerful leaders for centuries throughout history have used "food tasters" and employed other such extreme safety measures of screening their food and drink when President Roosevelt is naively accepting jars of Caviar and cases of Vodka from Stalin?!

The same Stalin who, Roosevelt remarked on page 103 in Shoumatoff book, murdered his own wife?

Shoumatoff's firsthand account of that conversation is as follows:

> "I asked if vodka was served at Yalta. "Oh yes, and I liked it very much. Stalin gave me a whole case, which I have in Washington, and also caviar which I brought here. It will be served tomorrow." Did you like Stalin?" I asked. Yes, he was quite a jolly fellow. But I am convinced he poisoned his wife! They seemed to be quite a nice crowd of people, except for a few sinister faces appearing here and there. I was rather amazed that he uttered this remark about Stalin, but I realized that he really felt that none of those present would repeat anything he said."

If you can get your mind past the idea of how incompetent President Roosevelt's Secret Service was that they would allow him to consume such gifts of food and drink during the biggest war the world had ever seen, and from a foreign leader no less, add this to your mental musings. Shoumatoff's photographer, who had full run of the house and grounds the day Roosevelt died, was using a phony name.

Nicholas Robbins was using an alias; his real name was Nicholas Kotzubinsky. The name change would have made any background check, or check as to the man's legitimacy or alliance to any number of the nation's enemies during the war, virtually impossible. In doing my research on Kotzubinsky, through a contact in Russia, I discovered facts about him and his family that were quite fascinating. Unfortunately, after several months of arguing with the people within the Russian archives, and prolonging the publication of the book in the process, I abandoned my aspirations of exposing what I had found.

What I can tell you is that when Kotzubinsky was granted his US nationalization papers he was encouraged by the reigning court justice to shorten his name. The name that he was given was Kobbins, which somehow, became Robbins within the next eighteen months of his life. Still think that FDR being poisoned was a laughable idea? Let me put it another way.

Here we have a sitting US President, in the midst of the biggest war in the world's history, accepting food and drink gifts from a foreign leader (who just happened to be one of the biggest murdering monsters in history), and who allowed his inner sanctum to be penetrated by a Russian man who his Secret Service couldn't have possibly cleared.

To be frank, I am amazed that FDR survived through his first three terms in office and lived long enough to be murdered in 1945. Nonetheless, murdered he was, and it was by lead poisoning. Lead poisoning is the only poisoning that accounts for all of the President's symptoms and the sudden onset thereof.

Literally every physical ailment/problem that FDR was having is a symptom of lead poisoning, and the list of effects of lead on the human body is the same today as it was in 1945. In fact, the President's symptoms were almost word for word and letter for letter the same. The official list of Lead poisoning symptoms are:

Cardiovascular

- Hypertension, elevated blood pressure
- Increased systolic blood pressure in men
- Cardio-toxic effects
- Increased risk of cardiovascular disease
- Coronary artery disease
- Anemia [lack of red blood cells, paleness]
- Platelet dysfunction
- Early death from heart attack or stroke

Intellectual and mental

- Cognitive function deficit
- Fatigue, muscular exhaustion
- Impaired concentration
- Depression
- Anxiety
- Personality changes
- Deficits in short term memory
- Sleep disturbance, insomnia

Sensory

- Abnormalities in fine motor control
- Abnormalities in vasomotor coordination
- Deficits in visual acuity
- Hearing loss

Gastrointestinal

- Weight loss/Loss of appetite
- Nausea
- Constipation, diarrhea
- Abdominal pain, cramps

Nervous system

- Encephalopathy [brain disease]
- Cerebrovascular stroke, cerebral hemorrhage
- Psychomotor impairment
- Nervous system impairment [AKA: wrist-drop]
- Peripheral Arterial Disease
- Slowed nerve conduction [slowed reaction time]
- Tremor

Skeletal

- Pallor (paleness, grey complexion)
- Bone marrow alterations
- Myalgia [muscle pain]
- Muscular weakness
- Arthralgia [joint pain]
- Wrist drop [the inability to extend the hand]
- Decreased longevity
- Adrenal dysfunction

- Renal damage

- Chronic lead nephropathy [kidney disease]

- Death from nephritis [kidney inflammation]

- Fanconi Syndrome [Renal Syndrome]

- Gout

- Renal hypertension

- Increase in creatinine concentration

It needs to be clearly stated at this point in the book that the misdiagnosis of these physicians had nothing to do with their negligence or inattentiveness toward the president's health. In fact Roosevelt's medical team was extremely diligent in their pursuit of an answer that, in 1945, simply wasn't available.

The knowledge of lead poisoning, and its effect on human beings, was not yet known in the United States during that time period. Think back to the television family *The Walton's*: would John Boy Walton or his family doctor on Walton's Mountain have known about such things? Of course not, such knowledge wasn't made common in America for several years after this event. It was, however, well known and understood throughout Europe.

In fact, in 1922 the League of Nations completely banned the use of lead-based paint for such reasons, but the United States failed to agree with or comply with the ban. Some progress was made in the United States in 1943, the year FDR began being poisoned, when a report concluded that children eating lead paint chips could suffer learning and intelligence issues. It wasn't until 1971 that lead paint was phased out in the United States when the nation passed the "Lead-Based Paint Poisoning Prevention Act."

The intentional lead poisoning of President Roosevelt between the years of 1943 and 1945 has been established as the only known poisoning agent that could cumulatively account for his mental and physical deterioration, and all of the other symptoms that he was having.

It even accounts for the yo-yo phenomenon of his being close to death and then rebounding to act like his old self again. Obviously, the yo-yo phenomenon occurred at times when the assassins' poison wasn't in the proximity of the President, and because of it his health began to rebound.

But why didn't the assassin just poison him with Warfarin as so many others had been during this time period? After all, Warfarin was the murder drug of the day. The answer was as ingenious as the selection of the poison itself, which was undetectable for the time period in this country.

It had to look as if FDR just slowly slipped away so no red flags would be raised. In fact, in numerous books on the subject it is repeatedly stated that the three doctors (Bruenn, Paulin and McIntyre) were in such agreement of what they thought had happened that no autopsy would be commissioned.

Why bother when he had been such a sick man? That was exactly what they were hoping for: full and complete acceptance without questions. Isn't that what happened in the history books? Again, for reasons stated earlier in the chapter, I will be quoting the book *FDR's Deadly Secret* to illustrate a few of the many examples of FDR's yo-yoing health.

> Page 83: ". . . his hemoglobin slipped back to 7.5 on May 17, only to rise again sharply to 8.75 on the 21st, again to 10.5 on the 24th, and to 12.0 on June 4th."

> Page 111: "...to complain of abdominal pain and tenderness associated with slight nausea. Despite treatment with injections of codeine, the pain persisted for three days, disappeared, then returned the following day."

Exactly how is this seesawing of Roosevelt's health explained despite the treatment of his doctor? Further confirmation of my exhaustive research was uncovered in the diary of President Roosevelt's cousin and confidant, Margaret (Daisy) Suckley. On page 203 of her now-published diary entitled *"Closest Companion,"* she included this startling comment from Doctor McIntyre.

> "It's the P's [President's] fourth day in bed, & he still feels somewhat miserable though his fever is gone. Last Tuesday without any warning, he felt ill at noon [AKA lunch time]. He lay on his study sofa & slept 'til 4:30pm. When he found he had a temp. of 102. The Dr. [McIntyre] found

it was a toxic poisoning, but they can't ascribe it to anything they know of."

Ok, stop, back up and read that last line again. The doctor actually mentions a mysterious toxic poisoning in reference to FDR's health and it's mentioned in Daisy's diary? Could there be a bigger smoking gun? She continues: *"they gave him 4 doses of a sulpha drug- from which he will have to recover."* Again, here is a doctor that is treating the result of the illness but not the cause of it. Also notice the time of the change in his health—lunchtime.

That type of continuous sickness had been the President's life for almost two years and the man was in agony. To my knowledge, no one has connected the dots like this, until I fully investigated both the medical and political aspects of the situation.

It took me almost four years to do, but when I was finished the whole situation became crystal clear. Numerous times from 1943 to 1945 I discovered reports of FDR suddenly becoming ill during or shortly after his meals. In fact these accounts are too numerous to list. Possibly the two best accounts are covered in *FDR's Deadly Secret* on page 91 and on page 110 respectfully

"...in Tehran, at the first summit meeting of the three major Allied leaders, during a steak and baked potato dinner that Roosevelt was hosting on November 28. He and Stalin were discussing the question of access to the Baltic Sea when, according to his interpreter, Charles Bohlen, "suddenly, in the flick of an eye, he turned green and great drops of sweat began to bead off his face; he put a shaky hand to his forehead."

"We were all caught by surprise…[Harry] Hopkins had the president wheeled to his room," where McIntire examined him. "To the relief of everyone, [Hopkins] reported [back] nothing more than a mild case of indigestion." Significantly though, "the President retired for the evening without returning to the dining room." Privately, Hopkins told Bohlen that "he was quite concerned."

"…and there was another disturbing sign: When a member of the British delegation asked Prime Minister Churchill whether Roosevelt had said much during that day's meeting with Stalin, he hesitated, then replied, "Harry Hopkins said that the president was inept. He was asked a lot of questions and gave the wrong answers."

"…his pressure was higher in the morning than at night. For example, on April 19 he woke with a pressure of 230/126-128; an hour later, after breakfast, it was 210/106. For unexplained reasons, Bruenn took another reading just five minutes later and found it had risen to 218/112. But in the evening, Roosevelt's pressure was at its lowest level of the day, a still alarming 190/90."

If you remember from a previous chapter, General Edwin "Pa" Watson mysteriously died on the return trip from the Yalta conference between the three Allied leaders as well. How coincidental. At this juncture the conclusion should be quite clear.

President Roosevelt was being intentionally and systematically reduced to a frail, shaky, and mindless man without the strength, endurance or mental capacity to lead the nation.

That question has been answered, but many more lie ahead. For starters, how was the lead entering FDR's body? Since lead is only poisonous to human beings through ingestion or inhalation, where was the poisoning coming from? Ingestion is the clear answer if you look at the evidence of FDR getting sick during mealtimes.

Obviously, President Roosevelt was ingesting lead in his food and drinks. It's the only possible option, but where was the President's food coming from? None other than Henrietta Nesbitt, the White House cook.

Upon investigation it seems that Mrs. Nesbitt is a very interesting person. A neighbor to the Roosevelts in Hyde Park, NY, and a close and very loyal friend to Eleanor Roosevelt, Mrs. Nesbitt was quite the political activist at the time when Franklin Roosevelt, then Governor of New York, was aspiring to be President of the United States.

It seems that her political initiative merged with Mrs. Roosevelt's at the forming of the local chapter of the League of Woman Voters, which on the surface seemed harmless enough, but the secret motive behind its formation at that time was to introduce Communism to the Governor's neighborhood.

This was an easy feat as the national headquarters of the Communist Party of the United States was, and still is, located on 23rd Street of New York City, just a little over an hour's ride by car.

At these meetings the two women were in agreement on the issues of women's empowerment, equality and other political affairs that they discussed both publicly and privately. Still, I felt that there was more to the story, so I drove the necessary 10 hours from my home to the Franklin D. Roosevelt Presidential Museum and National Archive in Hyde Park, NY.

It was my burning desire to dig into their archives and find whatever I could on Eleanor Roosevelt and her confidant, Henrietta Nesbitt. For anyone interested in visiting, the Franklin D. Roosevelt Presidential Museum and National Archive is quite a treat for the senses.

The grounds are beautifully manicured, and the newly renovated facility is impressive. The mansion itself is probably the most authentic building in the entire federal registry, as the Roosevelt family turned it over to the Parks Department a mere five years after President Roosevelt's death.

Adjacent to the mansion is President Roosevelt's museum, which also houses the Presidential library. Both will captivate visitors for hours with historic videos, exhibits and a period-specific timeline of the President's years in office.

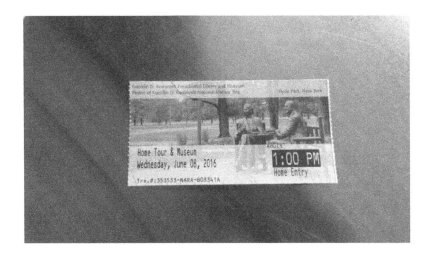

Ticket to the Presidential Library and Museum

President Roosevelt's mansion and boyhood home

Statues of President Roosevelt and the First Lady in the garden
at the Presidential Library and Museum.

It was during my visit to President Roosevelt's
museum itself that my suspicion of Eleanor Roosevelt's
questionable contacts were both amplified and
confirmed. While walking through the historical timeline
of Roosevelt's presidency, I was amazed to find the
First Lady's massive FBI file, which was on display in
the middle of the floor.

In fact, I almost fell right over it while I was looking at
another exhibit. This 38-inch-tall metal monster almost
put me in the emergency room. I couldn't help but
wonder why such an obstacle would be placed in
middle of the floor in that capacity.

Eleanor Roosevelt's massive FBI file
containing 3271 laminated pages
gathered by J. Edgar Hoover and the FBI
beginning in 1924 until her death in 1962

When I walked around the front of the obstruction and saw what it was, I finally understood its importance. Amazingly, it was exactly what I was looking for. Upon inspection of this oddly-placed exhibit I discovered that each page in her file was laminated and numbered, which was quite a feat for the entire contents of a three-drawer filing cabinet.

Although the signage attached to the exhibit itself is framed in words that would suggest that the contents were nothing more than "hearsay and gossip," J. Edgar Hoover had certainly been alerted by many people that she was a Communist, or at the very least a Communist sympathizer. All of her Communist activity was a foregone conclusion in my mind, but it still made my mental wheels spin out of control. While I thoroughly enjoyed the tour of the mansion, museum and the luxurious grounds, after seeing the filing cabinet and its contents, my next destination was an obvious one: The archives.

I knew that there had to more to the story, and if there was, I wasn't leaving until I found it. I now jokingly refer to my time investment of the next several hours in the Roosevelt archive as *"the death of an afternoon."* Their archive is located on the top floor of the museum almost directly over the exhibit that contains the custom-made President's car.

President Roosevelt's 1936 Ford Phaeton on display
within his presidential museum

As busloads of tourists, children on fieldtrips, and other curious history buffs were enjoying themselves on the floor beneath me, I remained sequestered away, neck deep in files and letters from FDR's three-and-a-quarter-terms in office. There I registered to view their massive cache of documentation that had been meticulously maintained by their friendly and attentive staff.

The author's official research card for the Franklin D. Roosevelt National Archives dated June 8th 2016.

It was difficult to ascertain exactly where to start, as there were over 17 million physical pages of documentation in the archives as well as 800,000 digitized documents and over 2,500 historical photographs. Entwined within this mountain of material were personal letters as well as papers from various individuals and organizations involved with the Roosevelts.

I could have spent the rest of my life in this gigantic archive and not seen half of the material that I was searching for if not for the help of the staff. Fortunately the archivist on duty was very helpful. Her name was Virginia, a very sweet woman, who took mercy on me after I told her that I was going to publish a book on Roosevelt. She never actually said so, but it was my feeling that it did her heart good to see someone actually using the archives for a real purpose as so many people were just wasting her time and being nosey.

She would never say such a thing but her actions gave me that impression as she very pleasant and very eager to help in any way that she could. She directed me to the files pictured below and it was there that I stuck the gold that I was digging for.

Photos of the author doing research in the national archives

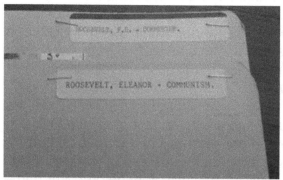

The President and the First Lady's files on their Communism

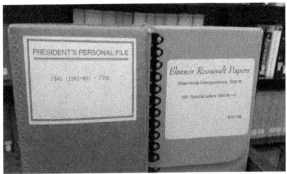
The Roosevelt's personal files, letters and correspondences

It didn't take me very long at all to uncover the fact that Eleanor Roosevelt was both an interesting and colorful character. In fact, while I was researching her numerous correspondences it became obvious that her contact with known Communist leaders, labor union infiltrators who were Communists, and others who were already under FBI investigation warranted the massive file that I had discovered previously in the museum below me.

The Communists and other questionable civil rights leaders that she had befriended spawned the FBI's in-depth investigation on her, which started in 1924 and continued for decades ending upon her death in 1962. You may ask yourself why the FBI investigation started in 1924?

Ironically, two things happened during this year that may have caught the FBI's attention. This was the same year that FDR returned to politics from his debilitating illness as he attended the Democratic National Convention, making the presidential nomination speech for the then-governor of New York, Al Smith.

Roosevelt and Smith had become very close over the 18 months prior to his candidacy. Unfortunately, Smith was already being investigated by the FBI, although erroneously, as being a Communist himself.

The second thing that happened during 1924 that may have caught the FBI's attention was the start of the close friendship and political involvement of Eleanor Roosevelt and Henrietta Nesbitt.

I will leave it up to the reader to decide whether these things were merely a coincidence, or if they gave the Federal Bureau of Investigation enough cause to warrant the file on Eleanor Roosevelt. Unfortunately, at this point, I believe that all we can do is speculate. I also uncovered numerous letters between President Roosevelt and Henrietta Nesbitt that were not pleasant. In fact, some were hostile.

They sparred repeatedly over the horrible food that the president had been receiving and which had been making him ill during or shortly after his mealtime. On one occasion he ordered her not to serve him sweetbreads until further notice.

This is an order that she ignored, resulting in yet another letter from the President which was not sent with good humor. On another occasion he told her when to pluck feathers from a goose, as the meat that he received was dry. The two of them went on like this for years. It was obvious that she was indeed punishing the president for his marital misdeeds and that she was disrespecting not only the man, but the office as well.

Shown below is a letter scolding Mrs. Nesbitt for ordering food from an outside source other than the market in Washington D.C. where she had been instructed to shop.

This was most curious. Why she was suddenly ordering food from an unidentified outside source? Did she really believe that the food wouldn't be rationed in other areas of the country? I found this public domain letter scolding Nesbitt to be most intriguing.

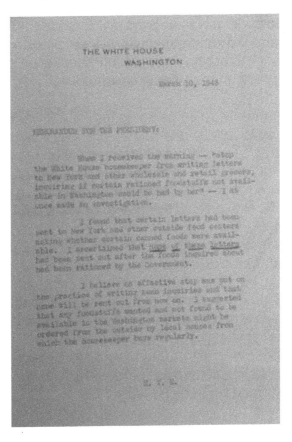

Coincidentally, the date of the letter was March 10th, 1943, the exact date that President Roosevelt began to have health issues, not to mention that she was trying to get food from New York as well as other *"outside food centers."* Wasn't the CPUSA located in New York? Conjecture? Possibly. Strange? Absolutely.

Other letters appeared between the First Lady and Mrs. Nesbitt, where they made references to their private conversations regarding *"other women"*. While the subject was couched in language that could be likened to code, it was beyond doubt to me that these notes made reference to conversations between Nesbitt and Eleanor about her long-running marital problems, and the president's extramarital affairs.

Unfortunately, rules being as they are, I wasn't given permission to publish the photos that I had taken of those letters. To this news I was greatly displeased, however, it was more than obvious that Mrs. Nesbitt became informed of the torturous private life that Eleanor Roosevelt was living at the hands of FDR.

When it came to extramarital affairs, President Roosevelt had a turnstile of willing suitors, but apparently had little interest in Eleanor. It seemed that FDR had time for every female except her, and when the couple went to the White House, the situation got worse. In Washington, FDR was secretly (and in some cases not-so-secretly) romancing almost every woman in the White House except for his wife. This made Mrs. Nesbitt's blood boil.

The very idea that her closest friend and confidant, the First Lady of the United States of America, was being forced to sleep in another bed and in another room made her furious.

Henrietta Nesbitt viewed President Roosevelt as an arrogant, chauvinistic bastard and she screwed with his food literally every chance she got. Indeed, Nesbitt was the very extension of her most loyal friend, employer and confidant, the First Lady.

Of the hours of research that I have done on the subject, two sources stood out as best describing the climate of angst and revenge that existed within the walls of the Roosevelt White House. The first work was written by Bob Carr, a columnist at the *Sydney Morning Herald*. He published an article on March 18, 2011, entitled "The Odd couple who changed America."

His article is one of the best written works that explains how Mrs. Nesbitt found pleasure in the torture of the president in every way possible, mainly through her cuisine. The second written work is an article written by Laura Shapiro in *The New Yorker* entitled "The First Kitchen." Her work was published on November 22, 2010.

Beginning with excerpts from Bob Carr's article, "The Odd couple who changed America," he writes: "Her cuisine was consistently awful. Runny porridge. Canned fruit. Watery soup. Gelatin salad with marshmallow. Franklin might have dismissed her, fed up with beans and boiled liver. But he would have overthrown "the first couple's hard-won balance of power," according to Eleanor's biographer, Blanche Wiesen Cook, who wrote in 1999 that Mrs. Nesbitt was part of Eleanor's "passive-aggressive tendencies" towards her husband."

"Missy LeHand, the president's stenographer, acted as his second wife. In the '20s, he would spend up to three months with her in a small cottage in Warm Springs, Georgia, a retreat to revive his diminished legs with the hot minerals. Meanwhile, back in New York, Eleanor ploughed progressive Democratic Party politics. In 1940, Franklin was dazzled by Princess Martha of Norway, welcomed as a White House guest. He was later to visit her in the Virginian hills - untroubled by press scrutiny - for whole afternoons."

"Between Franklin and Eleanor hovered his affair, from 1916 to 1918, when he was assistant secretary of the Navy, with Eleanor's young and graceful social secretary, Lucy Mercer. As president, after Lucy had been married and widowed, he revived the relationship. She was to be there at Warm Springs on April 12, 1945, when his head fell to one side and a stroke took his life, 82 days into his fourth term."

The evidence that Mrs. Nesbitt thoughts and deeds were truly an extension of Eleanor Roosevelt's is mounting against her. After reading the excerpts of Bob Carr's work, it appears obvious why Eleanor Roosevelt was conveniently missing when FDR was found dead at his cottage in Warm Springs, Georgia.

She had been living a life of separateness from her husband, a separateness that had been forced upon her by the president. By the time of FDR's death, Eleanor had little if any feelings remaining for the man. This more than explains why she shed virtually no tears upon receiving the news of his death and why Mrs. Nesbitt carried such aggression against the man.

Yes, she went through the motions of the presidential funeral with the necessary honor and dignity that so often accompanied her in everything that she did in the public's eye, but she was a victim at the hands of President Roosevelt whose actions both insulted and belittled her. The First Lady was a good woman and everyone who came in contact with her knew it to be true, especially Mrs. Nesbitt.

The next written work is an article written by Laura Shapiro in *The New Yorker* entitled "The First Kitchen." The following excerpts from her article both mirror those written by Mr. Carr and extend even further into the misgivings that happened behind the White House walls when America was none the wiser.

> Ms. Shapiro writes: "Meanwhile, both she and F.D.R. appear to have channeled their deepest emotions away from the marriage. F.D.R. had made a pet of his adoring secretary, Missy LeHand; he also secretly continued to see Lucy Mercer Rutherford. Eleanor had her own intimate friendships—precisely how intimate is unknown—with a reporter, Lorena Hickok, and a bodyguard, Earl Miller.

During those years, the Roosevelts had separate bedrooms and social lives, took separate vacations, ate most of their meals apart, and built their own Hyde Park cottages as getaways. "They had the most separate relationship I have ever seen between man and wife," J. B. West, a White House usher, wrote. "And the most equal." Blanche Wiesen Cook, who is currently at work on the third volume of her masterly biography of Eleanor, has called Mrs. Nesbitt "ER's revenge."

"Roosevelt, who had been raised on a Hyde Park estate with its own farm and fine cooks, knew the taste of excellent food and missed it badly. He didn't expect luxuries when the nation was in economic crisis, but he would have loved a decent fried egg and a cup of drinkable coffee. Mrs. Nesbitt finally gave him a coffeemaker so that he could brew his own, but this was a rare victory in a long series of skirmishes.

He made it clear that he disliked broccoli; Mrs. Nesbitt served it anyway. He ordered hot coffee for himself and a few guests; Mrs. Nesbitt sent up iced tea. He asked for canned white asparagus one day when he was sick; Mrs. Nesbitt insisted it wasn't available. (A secretary darted out and came back with ten cans.

"For the next twelve years, Mrs. Nesbitt turned out meals so gray, so drooping, and so spectacularly inept that they became a Washington legend. They also irritated an epicurean President three times a day—an outcome that may or may not have figured in Eleanor's calculations.

Numerous historians of the F.D.R. years have noted the abysmal meals at the White House, and anecdotes about Mrs. Nesbitt's assaults on the presidential palate have circulated in memoirs for decades." "Ernest Hemingway, invited to dinner at the White House in 1937, said that the food was the worst he'd ever eaten."

"We had a rainwater soup followed by rubber squab, a nice wilted salad and a cake some admirer had sent in. An enthusiastic but unskilled admirer," he wrote to his mother-in-law. He added that he now understood why the journalist Martha Gellhorn, a friend of Eleanor's who was also invited that night (and whom Hemingway married three years later), ate three sandwiches at the Newark airport while they were waiting for their flight. She dined with the Roosevelts frequently and told him that everybody in Washington knew the rule—when you're invited to the White House, eat before you go."

This wasn't a coincidence. Nor was it merely passive aggressive behavior by Mrs. Nesbitt, as previously mentioned. Hannibal Lecter couldn't keep this woman's food down. It was a pattern of behavior intended to embarrass, harass and humiliate President Roosevelt, every minute, of every day, and in front of every important guest and dignitary that he invited to the Presidential Mansion.

This was being carried out by a woman who was the First Lady's shill who knew that she couldn't be fired and could get away with anything that she wanted, anytime she wanted it. The more worthless and aggrieved the First Lady felt at the hands of the President, the worse the treatment of the president became.

Mrs. Nesbitt was evening the score, and that, my friends, supplies her with the Motive, Means and Opportunity to murder. Her food couldn't be that bad unless someone was trying to hide the ingestion of lead without detection, and if everyone's food was bad there would be no reason to investigate.

Any number of household or maintenance products contained lead during the 1940's, and some still do to this day. A spoonful of cleanser here, an ounce of floor wax there, and no one who was to be the wiser. Horrible food was the perfect cover. That's where the poisoning was coming from, but even the highly motivated and vengeful Mrs. Nesbitt couldn't just murder a president without it being detected.

There had to be another person involved in the plot. After all, where did the knowledge of lead poisoning come from? It couldn't have come from anyone inside of the United States of America, because the fact that lead was extremely toxic was unknown in this hemisphere and remained that way for years after President Roosevelt had been long dead.

Beyond the list of lead poisoning symptoms from earlier in the chapter, which perfectly matched all of Roosevelt's symptoms, and even looking beyond the numerous accounts of his health changing for the worse after or during mealtimes, are the numerous reports of his health bouncing from sickness to health and back to sickness again.

This is the work of an accomplice who is either a genius or someone who has been in close contact with someone else who has had a long history of poisoning someone slowly to avoid detection and/or alarm. The accomplice couldn't have been just anyone. There were certain elements and requirements to accomplish the deed that were necessary to meet.

To begin with, the accomplice had to be an Eleanor Roosevelt sympathizer who was fed up with the president's long-standing extramarital affairs and mistreatment of the First Lady during their marriage. In short, they had to side with Mrs. Nesbitt and share her distain for FDR. Next, the accomplice had to be someone with a full security clearance who was in the White House on a regular basis.

The accomplice also had to be someone who traveled abroad and came in contact with the knowledge that lead could be used as a poison. They had to know what contained it, where to find it, and know how to administer it so it would be both deadly and not raise any red flags. They also had to share the Motive, Means and Opportunity to murder. The accomplice is a name that you'll be familiar with.

6
The Requiem

"If any foreign minister begins to defend to the death a 'peace conference,' you can be sure his government has already placed its orders for new battleships and airplanes."

- Joseph Stalin -

Harry Hopkins is your accomplice, and his background is shocking. He held numerous positions in New York City working for governmental social organizations beginning in 1913 and working his way up the totem pole of responsibility to the federal level. This was an easy feat as his efforts were noticed by the Governor of New York State during that era. That governor was Franklin Roosevelt.

Hopkins started out as a mere acquaintance and political ally of Roosevelt as the two men found themselves in frequent proximity of the other. Roosevelt doled out the social programs and relied heavily on people like Hopkins to administer and oversee them.

It wasn't long before the two men became close friends and exited the restraints of the Empire State for the White House in Washington, D.C. Just as Eleanor Roosevelt exercised her spotlight cronyism by bringing her neighbor and political ally, Henrietta Nesbitt, to Washington, D.C., FDR did the same thing with Harry Hopkins. Eleanor Roosevelt and Henrietta Nesbitt already knew of Hopkins through his involvement with the newly formed Communist Party of the United States of America (CPUSA) which was established in 1919 and located in the middle of New York City. The establishment of the CPUSA was the brainchild of Woodrow Wilson's "alter ego" and closet Communist, Colonel Edwin Mandell House, who was the political idol of FDR.

At this time in America Communism was the new and exciting ideology that was being touted as the governmental end of all war, hunger, greed and strife. This was being fed to politicians and those in academia on the foresight and direction of Joseph Stalin, who at the time, was a member of the Russian Politburo alongside Lenin, Zinoviev, Kamenev, Trotsky, Sokolnikov and Bubnov.

Just as Stalin was twisting and manipulating those in his own country, he was doing the same thing overseas. Stalin knew that he was too far behind the West to overtake them industrially and too far away from them to conquer them militarily. His plan was obvious; he was going to overtake them from within, driven by his own political motivations.

His primary targets for his *Red Spread* were the countries that he feared the most, the Capitalist Democracies of the West. There he contacted leaders in academia, entertainment, government, labor unions, and civic policy and invited them to visit the Soviet Union and view their solution to the pitfalls of Capitalism.

Those invited came in droves and witnessed a phony town, likened to Main Street USA in Disney World, where Communism worked and everyone was happy and cared for. The guests were oblivious to the fact that, less than five miles outside of the cardboard town, hideous atrocities of injustice, poverty and murder were being committed.

During the visit each invitee was treated like royalty and sent home with instructions on how to start Communist Parties in their own country. Stalin convinced them that it was their duty to introduce this new and improved political ideology to their countries.

The literature that he gave his visitors upon their departure included, among other things, contact information allowing them to connect to those already planted with their countries and instructions on how to deliver funds to their Communist movement.

Stalin carefully warmed the pot, slowly convincing his new Communists that they were doing the right thing for their own countries, before bringing it to a boil where their members were leaking military secrets, influencing elections, and even committing murder, all for the Communist cause.

He had great aspirations of converting these countries, and, in doing so, overtaking their industries and turning them into Soviet satellite countries containing sleeper cells poised to aid in global domination. For Stalin, this was a do or die operation as he viewed the West as a direct threat.

This 1938 quote from Stalin shows his contempt for the countries of the West: "Russia must overtake the advanced capitalist countries in just ten years, or, I swear to you, those capitalist countries will destroy us." One of the people who was greatly influenced by Stalin's new ideology was the socially minded Harry Hopkins.

The Communists' lies of systematic success that were fed to the American government from 1920 until 1945 were extremely active behind the scenes of every program and policy written and enacted in our country, and in many respects, they still are. This fit in perfectly with FDR's "cradle-to-grave" idea of governmental support of its citizens, beginning with his reign in New York State and staying with him all the way to Washington.

According to a published article by George Washington University entitled "The Eleanor Roosevelt Papers Project, Teaching Eleanor Roosevelt Glossary," Mrs. Roosevelt and Harry Hopkins became very close as they worked together in the Capitol district of their political party. The article states the following: "In Albany, Hopkins and ER began an enduring friendship, which had significant impact on New Deal policy." This is where it all began, and their hero was Joseph Stalin.

Long before President Roosevelt and Harry Hopkins ever met Stalin in person he was their idol and they would cooperate and bend to his every whim. Although it was President Roosevelt who summoned Harry Hopkins to Washington, D.C., Hopkins was far better acquainted with Eleanor Roosevelt, Mrs. Nesbitt, and the organizing parties in the CPUSA.

In Washington, Franklin, Eleanor and Harry worked tirelessly to design and implement the first national relief organization which later came to be known as the Temporary Emergency Relief Administration (TERA). This and other expansions of the gigantic social and government control over the American public would have made their idol, Joseph Stalin, very happy.

It was during these years that Harry Hopkins, Henrietta Nesbitt, and Eleanor Roosevelt, all old friends, began to have talks long into the night about a variety of subjects that ranged from personal to political. Hopkins knew of the sadness that had become Eleanor's life and wasn't fond of the treatment that FDR had bestowed on her.

As the days of FDR's failed economic relief had turned into the war years, Hopkins acted as FDR's liaison abroad, implementing and administering the American Lend-Lease policy to Allied countries. In doing so he regularly traveled abroad establishing regular contact with foreign diplomats such as Winston Churchill, and his idol for decades, Joseph Stalin.

It was during these travels that Hopkins learned of the many forms of assassination by poison that had become commonplace in Europe, forms of assassination that hadn't reached the shores of America yet. It was the duty of the European governmental officials to inform Mr. Hopkins of such perils as his life may have been put in jeopardy by them. This is where the information came from to murder President Roosevelt.

Bill McIlvane of Historynet.com wrote a compelling article on August 19, 2000, entitled: "Lacking an official title for most of his years in Washington, Harry Hopkins came to be known as President Franklin D. Roosevelt's "Deputy President." "In the article he states the perils of Hopkins physical condition during this time.

He writes: "During the years 1941-1943, Hopkins could usually be found in his room at the White House, working in a bath-robe, with letters, papers, telegrams, and diplomatic dispatches strewn across his bed. It was common knowledge that Hopkins was desperately ill. In addition to the piles of official papers, his room was littered with medicines. He also was required to follow a strict diet that his wide-ranging activities made nearly impossible. Rexford Tugwell wrote that Hopkins seemed to hold himself together in 1943 through 'sheer nerve.'"

"As the war progressed, Hopkins' health grew progressively worse. His condition prevented his digestive system from absorbing enough fats and proteins, and Hopkins appeared more and more cadaverous despite regular blood transfusions.

"For Roosevelt and Hopkins, the February 1945 Yalta Conference was the last hurrah. Sadly, the two parted on a sour note. Exhausted and sick at the conclusion of the meetings, Hopkins decided to rest in Marrakech, Morocco, for a few days before returning to the United States. Roosevelt had expected Hopkins to return with him aboard the cruiser USS Quincy and help him write a speech on the results of the conference. Hopkins, however, insisted on staying behind, and their parting was not amicable."

Many questions arise from Mr. McIlvane's historical accounts but three stand out from the rest. 1) Why was Hopkins, a very sick man, leaving his White House residence? Hopkins' decision to suddenly seek shelter elsewhere happened in November of 1943.

That is not a matter of dispute; it is a matter of fact; what is a matter of dispute is why? Why move out of the White House and into a townhouse in Georgetown? The Hopkins exodus from the White House was indeed puzzling to everyone who worked there for many reasons.

It was in stark contrast to FDR's wishes. He wanted his closest friend and VIP as near to him as possible. FDR made no moves without Harry Hopkins' seal of approval so the move made no sense from that angle. Also, Hopkins was not a well man himself and FDR's doctor, Admiral Dr. Ross McIntire, was in the house frequently treating Roosevelt's various aches and pains and adjusting the President's leg braces.

While McIntire was at the White House he always treated the staff, other family members, and everyone who was in need of his medical attention, so there was no medical reason for the move. In fact free medical attention was incentive for Hopkins to stay, not leave.

The excuse given by Hopkins was that his newly married wife, his third wife, demanded a home of their own, but that turned out to be false as well. Neighbors to the relocated couple often recalled that she was unhappy there because "her Harry was so far away" when he was working long hours with Roosevelt at the White House.

Perhaps a hint of the sudden decision for Hopkins to exit the White House could be found elsewhere. Indeed it could. It was in November of 1943, just a month prior, that President Roosevelt's health began to visibly falter and his traditionally horrid food at the White House began to be tainted with lead. Hopkins' decision to exit was an obvious one. Harry was fleeing before people started asking in-depth questions regarding the President's deteriorating health.

2) Why did Hopkins abandon FDR immediately after the Yalta Conference? What was driving the sudden need to separate himself first from the White House and then from the President himself?

This behavior is quite odd for a man who was of the most trusted and highest level of confidants to the president and the First Lady for over a decade. He left right then? Why? If he was indeed feeling ill there were many doctors on board the ship that could have attended to him.

3) Who was Mr. Hopkins to defy the wishes of the Commander in Chief? After all, FDR held the highest office in the country. For a man (Hopkins) without a real title to defy the wishes of a sitting US President would certainly result in a penalty of some variety, right?

Apparently not. In fact, the split between the men was so divisive that it is reported that they never spoke to each other or saw each other again. The answers to these questions are obvious. Harry Hopkins was no longer taking orders from President Roosevelt; he was taking orders from Stalin.

Oleg Gordievsky, a prominent Soviet K.G.B. defector and author of the book *K.G.B.: The Inside Story*, identified Harry Hopkins as "the most important of all Soviet wartime agents in the United States." This information was again confessed to *The New York Times* writer Craig R. Whitney and appeared in the 1990 article entitled: "Roosevelt Aide Called an Unwitting Spy."

The article details the information revealed in his new book but the title of the newspaper piece was in error. There was nothing "unwitting" about the treachery of Harry Hopkins.

On June 6th, 2013, Robert Stacy McCain, a veteran journalist and contributor to *The Washington Times* shared the following research into the investigation of Harry Hopkins. After years of investigation into the matter Mr. McCain wrote the following: "A confidential message from FBI Director J. Edgar Hoover, reproduced in [Diana] West's new book, told [White House aide Harry] Hopkins that a 'continuing' investigation had discovered that Russian diplomat (and Comintern agent) Vasily Zarubin had made a payment to U.S. Communist Party official Steve

Nelson to help place espionage agents 'in industries engaged in secret war production."

... so that information could be obtained for transmittal to the Soviet Union.' This information had come from a 'bug' at Nelson's home in Oakland, California, through which the FBI first learned of the Soviet effort (code-named 'Enormous') to obtain the atomic secrets of the Manhattan Project. Instead of warning President Roosevelt, however, Hopkins 'privately warned the Soviet embassy in Washington that the FBI had bugged a secret meeting' between Nelson and Zarubin, according to documents from the KGB archives smuggled out by [former Soviet intelligence officer Vasili] Mitrokhin."

Harry Hopkins? An *"unwitting"* spy? Hardly. Harry Hopkins was identified in the decades that followed the World War II era as the mysterious "Agent 19" who contacted a Soviet covert operative named Iskhak Akhmerov.

These messages revealed top secret information on the Venona Project. Venona was the name of a successful project to decipher coded Soviet transmissions between Soviet intelligence stations in New York, Washington, London, and numerous other locations around the globe. The gathering point of the coded messages was none other than the Soviet capital, Moscow.

The Soviets' highly sophisticated code was very refined and largely unbreakable, but an error made by two individuals during the transmission process resulted in the deciphering of thousands of cable transmissions between the years of 1942 through 1946. Having great faith in their encryption and their advanced cipher, Soviet Intelligence used code names and even real names in their coded messages in the later years of the war.

There on a page numbered 812, is "agent 19", Harry Hopkins, sending a cable from the New York station of the NKVD (later to evolve into the KGB) which operated out of the Soviet diplomatic consulate in New York City. The date of the transmission was May 29, 1943. The same time that Harry Hopkins had his sudden revelation to change his residence and move out of the White House. It is impossible for this to be a coincidence.

Why? Along with the Venona project information were quotes from private discussions between President Roosevelt and British Prime Minister Winston Churchill. There is only one person on planet earth that had free and ready access to that information: Harry Hopkins.

Author extraordinaire and noted Communist researcher Diana West wrote a five-part series of articles based on her new book, *American Betrayal: The Secret Assault on Our Nation's Character*. The first of these articles was published on August 5, 2013 on the Breitbart news site and was entitled: "Did the Roosevelt Administration Send Uranium and Other Atomic Materials to Stalin?"

If any question remains about who Harry Hopkins really worked for, Diana West quashes them. She writes: "We certainly aren't taught that Lend Lease, perhaps even Hopkins himself, pushed uranium and other A-bomb essentials through to Stalin. These uranium shipments, erased from our historical memory but documented by Congress in 1950, took place at a time when the atomic development program known as the Manhattan Project was, we thought, our most precious secret."

Why would Lend Lease, overseen by Hopkins — who was also, not coincidentally, FDR's liaison to atomic research — do such a thing? The answer may relate to something else we don't learn about Harry Hopkins: FDR's powerful wartime advisor may have been a Soviet agent — and "the most important of all Soviet wartime agents. This was the estimation of Iskhak Ahkmerov, the famed Soviet *"illegal"* who ran a stable of top spies for the Kremlin, including Alger Hiss.

Oleg Gordievsky, a former KGB colonel and trusted defector, reported in his 1990 book *KGB*, co-authored with Christopher Andrew, that he heard Akhmerov single out Hopkins as the Soviets' No. 1 agent in a lecture to KGB officers in the 1960s."

Once again, the date of Harry Hopkins' (Agent 19) treachery against the United States was the same approximate time that his cable transmission to Moscow was discovered decades after his death, the date was in 1943. In fact, it was May 12th 1943. Five short months later Harry Hopkins decided to stage a surprise exodus from his longtime residence at the White House.

The more I began to dig into Harry Hopkins the more there was to dig into. I felt like I was peeling an onion, layer after layer, peel after peel, and it made my eyes burn. Yet reality had to hit me at some point during my investigation into President Roosevelt's murder. Hopkins secretly working for Stalin and sending cable spy transmissions, facts and events that couldn't have been uncovered for years into the future, simply wasn't enough to hit the home run.

After all, Hopkins was a dying man and those secrets wouldn't have been investigated, let alone discovered, until long after his death. There had to be a more compelling motive that would convince Hopkins to suddenly take up residence elsewhere.

After mulling over the dates once again it finally hit me. 1943 was the very time that FDR's health began to slide for reasons that his doctors couldn't identify. Everyone was concerned, everyone was curious and everyone was baffled. Desiring to remove himself from being a White House resident and reside in a townhouse in Georgetown, Hopkins removed himself from being caught in a collusion to tamper with the president's food.

Unbeknownst to the First Lady, Mrs. Nesbitt, the White House cook, and Harry Hopkins, the president's most trusted foreign advisor, had conspired to kill President Roosevelt. Each had their own reasons. Nesbitt hated Roosevelt and loathed his infidelity. She knew that FDR had many affairs within the White House at the expense of her best friend, the First Lady.

She saw FDR for the swaggering and pompous Casanova that he was, all at the emotional expense of Eleanor. Nesbitt grew tired of seeing the First Lady internally tormented by FDR's extramarital affairs and externally tormented by those around her as they laughed up their sleeves at her. Hopkins had his own agenda.

As Stalin's primary spy within the White House there was scarcely a branch of FDR's government that did not have moles in high places that were feeding Moscow with inside information. Hopkins oversaw the communication of two agents, named Whittaker Chambers and Elizabeth Bentley, who ran such a huge spy ring that literally every branch of the United States government had been infiltrated.

When Chambers and Bentley defected to the United States and ended their Soviet spy activities, they revealed hundreds of their fellow informants within the Federal government. Below are some of the more high profile informants.

Lee Pressman:
AAA (Agricultural Adjustment Administration).

John Abt:
WPA (Works Progress Administration), LaFollette Committee, U.S. Attorney General's Office.

Marion Bachrach:
Minnesota Farmer-Labor Party.

Alger Hiss:
AAA (Agricultural Adjustment Administration), Nye Committee, Department of State.

Donald Hiss:
Department of State.

Nathan Witt: AAA (Agricultural Adjustment Administration), NLRB(National Labor Relations Board).

Victor Perlo:
War Production Board, Price Administration, US Treasury Dept.

Charles Kramer:
Manager of the Department of Labor.

George Silverman:
Transport, U.S. Tariff Commission, Labor Advisory Board.

Henry Collins:
National Recovery Administration, AAA (Agricultural Adjustment Administration).

Nathaniel Weyl:
AAA (Agricultural Adjustment Administration). John Herrmann: AAA (Agricultural Adjustment Administration).

Harry Dexter White:
Monetary Research, Treasury Department.

Harold Glasser:
Monetary Research, Treasury Department. Noel Field:
Department of State.

Julian Wadleigh:
Agriculture, Department of State. Vincent Reno: U.S.
Army, Ward Pigman: National Bureau of Standards,
Public Welfare Committee

It was information from this network of informants
and his many trips to foreign countries that provided
Harry Hopkins with the knowledge that lead was a
method of poisoning that was not just unheard-of, but
was also completely undetectable in the United States
at that time.

Doubtless Hopkins informed Mrs. Nesbitt that any
household cleaner, polisher or solvent contained a
sufficient amount of lead to kill the president slowly and
without detection. The lead in combination with her
already horrible cuisine would provide the perfect cover
to the crime.

There is little doubt that when President Roosevelt
finally died in in 1945 that he had more cumulative lead
in his system than a battleship. Hopkins, knowing that
FDR's demise would be a long and slow process,
ensured the fact that his death would appear natural
and when it happened, he would be far apart from the
man.

The excuse he gave Mrs. Nesbitt for leaving the
White House, that his wife wanted her own house, was
nothing more than a planted cover story to leave her
holding the bag. If anyone were caught at that point

then Hopkins would be free and protected by FDR's friendship. It was the perfect plan, and it worked perfectly. Ironically Hopkins was also a dying man suffering from digestive issues who had battled ill health throughout the last three years of his life. Pushing irony to the very brink of reason, all of Hopkins issues were also symptoms of lead poisoning.

Let your mind feast on that for a moment and consider the following: in the same way that Jack Ruby shot Lee Harvey Oswald so he wouldn't talk after the assassination of President Kennedy, was Stalin remotely and slowly killing Hopkins for the same reason? As we learned with the aftermath of the Kennedy assassination, all loose ends would have to be trimmed when a president is murdered.

For my official investigation on the JFK assassination you will want to buy *Who Murdered JFK?*. I have a rare opportunity of knowing everyone from Mark Lane, who was the first to reveal the legal conspiracy in 1964, to Steve Jaffe who physically brought the Zapruder film to America from France where it was housed. You will be both surprised and delighted by this upcoming book. Be sure not to miss it.

In the case of Stalin and Hopkins, was this happening? Obviously this is only a theory and there is no proof to substantiate this claim, but it is entirely possible. In fact I believe that it's glaringly obvious. Stalin was a hideous, murdering monster, but he wasn't stupid.

On the morning of Thursday, April 12th, 1945, President Roosevelt was on a retreat in his favorite place on earth: Warm Springs, Georgia. The president ate a light breakfast and prepared for his afternoon barbecue. He also planned a visit to see some of the children who were rehearsing for a minstrel show that he would be attending.

Daisy Bonner, the cook at the Little White House, was by far his favorite and was a welcome change from the passive aggressive food torture that he had to endure at the hand of Mrs. Nesbitt. In reality this was probably the only food that the man was eating that wasn't loaded with lead.

This explains the see-saw that had become the president's health during the last few years of his life and more than explains why he always returned from Warm Springs a far healthier man than when he arrived. It was no coincidence that the person painting his portrait that afternoon was Elizabeth Shoumatoff, or that Shoumatoff's client list read like the "who's who" of Roosevelt haters who wanted him dead.

Aside from her gigantic client list, which was covered in Chapter 4, she writes the following quote in her book: "Not only her portraits, but also Elizabeth herself, were often seen in Bar Harbor to Palm Beach, from Cape Cod, Newport, and Sea Island to Wyoming, Texas and Hawaii; she was especially well known in Wilmington, Baltimore, Washington, Winston-Salem, Atlanta, Pittsburgh, and Akron, as well as in Long Island and New York.

Her work is a unique record of a noteworthy but private segment of American life. She also painted in Canada, England, Belgium, Luxembourg, Italy, and Liberia. Because of her keen interest in others and her great vitality, many of her subjects became close, lifelong friends."

She was certainly close and lifelong friends with a tiny army of people who not only hated the president, but who also had the money and the power to arrange his death and make it look like an accident.

Shoumatoff herself was an interesting character. She was a proud Russian and the daughter of General Nicholas Avinoff. Born near Kharkow in the Ukraine her family was affluent and held high governmental stature. As a girl her family lived in a spacious country house called Shindeyevo during the spring and summer months and in the late fall they relocated to their retreat in St. Petersburg.

According to her book she "…came to America with her husband Leo, who was on a mission for the provisional government headed by Alexander Krensky." Although no one has ever been told or has ever been able to determine exactly what his mission for the Russian government was, one can only surmise.

What is known about the couple is that, during the early years of their American defection, they, along with their three children, bounced around a few small towns in Upstate New York before finally settling in Long Island.

There Leo Shoumatoff, Elizabeth's husband, found work as a business manager with the Sikorsky Aviation Corporation. This is an interesting coincidence, as the company was founded and owned by another defected Russian living in America, aviation genius, Igor Sikorsky.

What is not known is how Shoumatoff and Sikorsky met. That seems to be as big a mystery as how his wife, Elizabeth, met and befriended Nicholas Kotzubisky, another defected Russian living in America under the alias of Nicholas Robbins.

It was been widely rumored that all of these people were either Russian spies or Russian operatives. Could that have been the governmental mission that Leo Shoumatoff was sent to America to accomplish? If not, how did all of these defected Russians in a country as large as the United States of America find each other?

While I don't believe that Elizabeth Shoumatoff was sent to murder the president, she was there to bear a true witness to the health of FDR and report what she had seen to Stalin, her husband's contacts, as well as to her laundry list of clients that despised him. There were many reasons this needed to happen.

The first of these reasons was an obvious one for any capitalist during the 1940s. They knew that FDR's restrictions, regulations, price fixing and his steady flow of Progressive/Liberal policies were a wet blanket on the economy, and they were trying to get inside information as to when he would die so they could buy in and time the market for maximum profits. The real money people needed to know inside information then just like they seek it today. In that realm nothing has changed. The second of these reasons was more secretive. With FDR and Hopkins no longer in the same company, Stalin needed a report on the condition of the president's health.

This was necessary for him to enact his finely crafted plan of the post-war land grab, which would, hopefully, lead to Communist world domination. Stalin's timing needed to be perfect and he needed as much information as possible.

Stalin was a true mastermind of both political and military strategy. He was cunning, crafty and had the ability to see around corners using nothing more than his gut and his intuition. He also had a vast global spy network. The big question is why? Why would Stalin want to kill FDR when he gave him almost, if not everything, he ever wanted or asked for?

From the very beginning Stalin viewed the United States and England as temporary allies – nothing more. Stalin, who was clearly in the strongest position throughout the Allied negotiations, had cast many fears in the hearts and minds of both President Roosevelt and his British counterpart, Prime Minister Winston Churchill.

At the time, Russia had the strongest army, the best leadership and a ruler who had three times the balls of any other leader on earth. Stalin clearly had his eye on the post-war world and had his own plans to spread his Communist empire throughout as much of Europe and Asia as humanly possible. Stalin viewed the war-torn world as easy prey for his Communist machine to conquer and rule. This sentiment is mirrored in the History Channel documentary *The World Wars*. The documentary quotes the following:

> "President Roosevelt is beginning to fear that if Joseph Stalin defeats Adolph Hitler alone he'll conquer Europe for himself, replacing one tyrant with another.

> Roosevelt knows that he needs to get the Americans into Europe as quickly as possible. He sends an allied force into Sicily hoping to conquer the island so he can establish a base of operations to launch an attack against the Axis powers in Europe."

> "Roosevelt and Churchill know that Stalin is a brutal tyrant who shares more in common with Hitler than with them. But they come to the realization that the enemy of their enemy needs to be their friend and if the Allies are going to win this war they need Stalin on their side."

There are two reasons that FDR gave Stalin everything that he wanted in every negotiation (much to the chagrin of Churchill): the first reason was fear. Roosevelt was horrified that if Stalin mobilized his massive Russian army against the US that he would completely overrun the western hemisphere.

Compounding FDR's fear of the Russian military might was the country's geographical location. FDR knew that the massive population of Russia could easily overrun all of the helpless European countries as well as most of Asia.

Knowing this, FDR set out to appease Stalin in the same way that Chamberlain tried to appease Hitler. FDR knew that the easiest way to keep America, as well as the other countries, from complete Communist domination under Stalin's rule was to treat him as his best friend and suck up to him as much as possible. Roosevelt, who was capable of magnificent insincerity, excelled at both tasks.

The second reason that President Roosevelt gave Stalin everything that he desired was envy. Stalin was Roosevelt's hero. Stalin had complete and total control over the entire country and all of its internal workings which was something that FDR was amorously infatuated with. Total and complete control of the United States was something that interested Roosevelt a great deal.

Throughout his entire presidency he was able to control the means of production, much like Stalin, with his New Deal initiatives, but dealing with the other party was a chore. FDR dreamt of the control that Stalin had where he wouldn't have to "pack courts", get permission to wage war or have his Second New Deal struck down. Roosevelt was following in Stalin's footsteps and he was learning along the way.

In fact, one historian went so far as to say that FDR was nothing more than a Stalin wannabee. During FDR's term in office America was dangerously close to becoming a Communist dictatorship. Why did Stalin want FDR murdered?

At the 1943 Tehran Conference, President Roosevelt told Stalin of his plan for the "Big Four" countries to act as the world's "Four Policemen." Those four were the United States, Britain, China and the Soviet Union. He envisioned their job as policing the world to disarm aggressor states. This post-war council was FDR's idea to guarantee world peace.

FDR further envisioned a United Nations that would consist of three branches, similar to the three branches of government that had previously existed in the United States prior to his inauguration, the same three branches that he wasted no time in monopolizing.

In the UN the "Big Four" would be active in two of the branches: the executive branch and the enforcement branch where they would police the hemispheres, with the third being an international assembly representing the member nations.

This is NOT what Stalin wanted. Yalta was a disaster for Roosevelt as well as America. The president was too trusting of Stalin, and couldn't comprehend the fact that the dictator didn't have the same vision of the world that he did.

He couldn't understand that Stalin did not reciprocate America's good faith. Stalin was a paranoid, power-hungry dictator who wanted to rule the world—not share it. Stalin, who was always fascinated by manpower, was sizing up the country of China for a future invasion.

His future plan was to expand his Communist empire into the islands of the South Pacific and to then surround China, overtaking and replacing their Leninist leader, Mao Tse-tung. With China being one of Roosevelt's "Four Policemen," Stalin's plans would not have been possible.

The History Channel documentary, *The World Wars*, covers this in remarkable detail.

> "McArthur is not the only one with plans for the conquest of Japan. As the war nears an end Joseph Stalin looks to take control. In July of 1945 Stalin begins mobilizing his troops into China. He's not about to let the United States have Japan for themselves, and he believes that if he can beat America to the punch, his power on the world's stage will be unmatched."

By taking control of the Pacific Ocean his future invasion of America, as well as China, could become a reality. This Communist ambition came into being in the early 1960s under Stalin's successor, Soviet Premier Nikita Khrushchev.

It is no coincidence that immediately after this conference in 1943 Harry Hopkins exited the White House and President Roosevelt's health began to falter. Hopkins and Stalin needed to make the poisoning look like a natural illness. The timing was perfect. Stalin knew approximately how long it would take lead poisoning to kill FDR, and he also knew that it would happen as the war was ending. The second reason Stalin needed to murder President Roosevelt came in 1945. In February of that year the three Allied leaders met again at the Yalta Conference. There, with FDR nearly lead poisoned to death and only days from his grave, Joseph Stalin was being pressured to allow free elections for the countries in Eastern Europe. Stalin hated the idea but agreed because he knew that FDR wouldn't live long enough to enforce it.

The Red Army had conquered a great expense of land and Stalin was unwilling to simply withdraw, allowing the western-style governments to push right up to its borders. Stalin knew that because the Soviet Union had no secure rivers, mountains, deserts or seas, it could easily increase its size by adding war torn towns and creating a new border.

This was desirable to Stalin to expand his Communist empire, but he also wanted to push the country's border as far away from its heartland of Moscow and Minsk as possible. Having an enemy penetrate as far into the Russian heartland as Hitler had was something that Stalin knew needed to be avoided at all costs in the future. Stalin adapted the underlying Marxist ideology which claimed that a Communist Revolution was inevitable.

The Soviet Union saw it as their mission to export their revolution to other countries. The countries of Albania, Poland, Romania, Hungary, East Germany, Czechoslovakia, and Bulgaria had been gobbled up by the Soviets and established Communist governments. This was Stalin's plan all along—to expand his empire. The evolution of this seven-satellite country buffer zone was the Warsaw Pact of 1955.

The pact was a defense alliance that put the Soviet Union in command of the armed forces of these member states. According to the treaty, member states would come to the defense of any member attacked by an outside force, setting up a unified military command under the Soviet Union.

The seeds that Stalin planted in 1945 would grow into a dream come true for him just ten years later. None of this would have been possible with Stalin agreeing to free elections.

Obviously Stalin said one thing at the bargaining table to make everyone happy and greatly desired another. The third reason that Stalin needed to murder President Roosevelt was leverage.

Stalin was arrogant. He knew that he was the most powerful man in the world, and he viewed Churchill and the UK as tiny specks on the map that he could squash like a bug. He also knew through his ever-expanding Communist Party and their network of spies in England, how fragile Britain was during the war and how desperately they needed to be rescued by the United States.

Stalin had other plans for Churchill, which I will discuss later in this chapter, but assassination wasn't among them. Of the three Allied powers Stalin knew that FDR was his biggest threat, and his biggest stumbling block to his goal of global domination.

Stalin was in the strongest position in the negotiations and managed to con the Allies by telling them that if the Soviets invaded Germany without them then he wouldn't need them or their help.

This was an outcome that left Roosevelt and Churchill shaking in their shoes, as the expansion of the Soviet Union into all the German regions would replace one brutal dictator with another.

America helping Stalin by landing in France was a far bigger accomplishment than Russia helping America defeat the Japanese in the South Pacific. The entire negotiation was a tilted toward Stalin's side as he pressured Roosevelt to invade.

This had nothing to do with Stalin's concerns of saving the lives of his soldiers, as he was one of the biggest mass murderers in history, slaying millions of his fellow Soviets without a second thought. He wanted to save his military and their armament for global takeover.

He also wanted to see what military might America would be able to muster. He wanted to size up the military competition. To Stalin, World War II was just a warm up for what he was planning. He already knew through his internal operatives and spy network that the United States was too big overthrow in a political coup, but after June 6, 1944 he began getting nervous as he became impressed with America's military power.

Knowing that President Roosevelt commanded an army with enough military might to give the Soviets a bloody nightmare didn't set well with him. Combine this knowledge with his inside information of "the bomb" from Agent 19, and he knew that the balance of power in the world was beginning to tilt toward the U.S. This was something that Stalin couldn't have.

Stalin knew that President Roosevelt was a skilled negotiator and with Roosevelt's command of such a powerful army, Stalin would have to behave, and behaving meant staying in his place. Stalin wanted no part of that. There was no second guessing this; FDR had to go.

Through his vast spy network in America, Stalin had learned that President Roosevelt's Vice President was a political newcomer. A shriveled little man with thick glasses whose only experience in life was being a shop keeper from Missouri. With FDR murdered, Stalin felt certain that he could bulldoze such a nerdy little man.

I have long said that every aggressor needs a victim, and Joseph Stalin's victim was soon to be Harry Truman. It was designed to be. The final reason that Stalin wanted to have FDR murdered was due to his underlying personality.

He had been murdering people and backstabbing political and personal allies his entire life. There was evidence of a pattern of behavior stemming back to his twenties as an exiled comrade of the Russian Revolution.

Among the murdered were his wife, personal physician, numerous political allies in the Politburo and finally his mentor Vladimir Lenin. This was how he rose to power, maintained power and built upon his power. This was normal for him.

Stalin was born on December 18, 1878, in the town of Gori in the Tiflis Governorate of the Russian Empire. This region today is known as the country of Georgia.

His birth name was Loseb Besarionis dze Jughashvili and he was born into a poor family. His father was a part time cobbler who struggled to find work and slid into alcoholism and abuse. His mother was a housemaid and launderer who was frequently beaten by her husband in their sagging two room existence.

Childhood greeted Ioseb with numerous health issues and a face that was permanently scarred by smallpox. He also injured his left arm in a farming accident leaving it shorter and stiffer than the other. He was soon enrolled in an Orthodox priesthood school at his mother's behest, but her struggle for family normalcy was cut short as her husband separated from her to live in another town.

Ioseb left the priesthood an atheist, becoming a voracious reader and a Georgian cultural nationalist. The school remembered him as being involved in student politics, unable to pay his tuition and that he was expelled after missing his final exams.

After his failing at the school he discovered the writings of Vladimir Lenin and joined the Russian Social-Democratic Labour Party, a Marxist group. He joined Lenin and was able to fight and rob trains and banks to fill the party coffers.

He soon had a reputation of someone who could get things done. This reputation led to him being branded with his new name of Stalin, which translates to "man of steel." He was constantly arrested by the Russian czar's police force and languished in exile in Siberia.

Not an intellectual like the rest of Lenin's followers, he became their enforcer in the field in the Russian civil war where class struggle for him involved the fist. With the revolution, he found favor with Lenin, and became party secretary.

Stalin was one of the members of the first Politburo and managed the Bolshevik Revolution with his six revolutionaries: Lenin, Zinoviev, Kamenev, Trotsky, Sokolnikov and Bubnov. As General Secretary of the party's Central Committee he kept journals and appointed people to key positions.

Craving power and eyeing an eventual takeover of the government, he was very careful to fill these positions with people who agreed with him and his philosophies. Stalin's wife worked in Lenin's office and she was a very involved Communist. Her eyes and ears were everywhere.

When she came home at night Stalin wanted to know everything Lenin did or said. Stalin's curiosity wasn't devotion, he was using his wife as an unwitting spy. Stalin's use of her information was a pattern that he would later employ on how to win the party over. Stalin spent hours memorizing Lenin's words and mannerisms.

He would study whole paragraphs and memorize them so that he knew them by heart, but it was not devotion, it was ammunition. Lenin said there must be no divisions in the party but each time Kemanov, Trotsky, and Znoveov made a speech, Stalin found a way of using Lenin's words against them.

Quoting some little phrase and twisting its meaning, so the party would vote his way, Stalin packed the party with his supporters until he and the party line became one. Stalin knew that in order to take control of the country he needed to turn the people on his biggest rival.

To accomplish this he would form the anti-Trotsky alliance with two of his fellow Politburo members; Kemanov and Znoveov. Like most of his alliances, it wouldn't last. Stalin had a lifelong history of making temporary allies of people, using them to his full benefit, and then killing or discarding them.

Lenin's wife, Krupskaya, had no love for Stalin. She said he was no real Bolshevik, claiming that he only wanted power for its own sake. She hated him because he'd used Lenin's memory and twisted it to win power. She said that by the end Lenin could see that Stalin was no good.

In Lenin's will he wrote "Comrade Stalin is too rude, too dangerous, remove him." Krupskaya added that Trotsky, Komanov, and Znoveov thought Stalin was a mere nothing and had many names for him. They laughed at Stalin behind his back and called him "comrade filing card", "pen pusher" and "the grey blur."

Viewing Stalin as no threat, they ignored Lenin's words where he evaluated each of the party's members so painstakingly penned for the party's future. Kemanov and Znoveov stayed loyal to Stalin after the will was read.

He thought that he was going to need their devotion to stay in his position, but after there was no impact from Lenin's will and Stalin remained as general secretary, he immediately turned on them. In 1926 Stalin switched gears and allied himself with the conservatives and Nikolai Bukharin, using him to kick Kemanov and Znoveov out of the Politburo.

When that feat was accomplished, he turned on the conservatives and ousted them as well. All the while he was backfilling these vacant positions with his political cronies. He continued to twist and spin his way through the government until he was able to demote Trotsky, his biggest rival, and force him into exile.

Trotsky was never allowed in Russia again, and while the remaining Leninists fought and quarreled with each other Stalin was able to dispose of them one by one until he was the absolute ruler. In the *BBC Two* documentary, *The Soviets: Stalin Takes Control*, Nikolai Bukharin is quoted as saying "Stalin knows only vengeance, the stab in the back."

This was the mark of a political and strategic genius. Stalin was the lion dressed as the sheep. With the contents of Lenin's Last Will and Testament kept quiet, Stalin turned Lenin's death to his political advantage. Krupskaya wanted a simple burial, but Stalin turned Lenin into a cult.

He had his body embalmed and built a tomb for him in Red Square. There his words were printed in bulk as though he a religious leader surrounded by his texts. While all this publicity was going on, Stalin played the part of his humble disciple.

In truth, Stalin the ruler, was a far more vicious and hideous man than the rebel who contorted his way to accomplish it. The worst thing Joseph Stalin could ever do to someone is befriend them or marry them. People had a nasty habit of getting dead around him, starting at the turn of the twentieth century, up to and including President Roosevelt in 1945. Ekaterina Svanidze (Kato as she was called) was Stalin's first wife.

She died in 1907 after only 18 months of marriage. The official cause of death of the twenty-two year old bride was typhus, but no official records remain. Stalin would disown their only son who was brought up by his wife's family. Leon Trotsky was exiled from Russia only to be hunted down and murdered in Mexico City by Ramón Mercader. Mercader was an assassin of Stalin's who murdered Trotsky with an axe.

Stalin's second wife, Nadezhda Alliluyeva, became unhappy with her daily grind, and became a student at the institute of commerce. There she learned from other students that millions were dying due to the famine, and that a war on the peasantry was being waged. She learned that her husband was forcing farmers onto huge state-run farms to increase production, and butchering their sheep and cows for the upper class.

The food supply to workers had dried up and requisition squads were called in to seize food, taking everything. They even took the grain to sow for next year's harvest. There was nothing left. They had long since eaten the cats and dogs.

To even speak of the famine was an offense punishable by 3-5 years of hard labor. When she questioned Stalin about what was happening she was found shot through the head. At the funeral Stalin said "She died my enemy."

Soon after Stalin had his personal doctor, Professor Dimitri Pletnov, murdered. Each day Pletnov massaged Stalin's body and tested his food for poison. Eventually other members of the Politburo would come in and talk freely, none of them minding what they said in front of the doctor. Horrible stories were shared.

Almost immediately the doctor was alerted to a newspaper article in the *Pravda* (the Russian word for truth). The article had been planted by Stalin damning Pletnov as a sadistic doctor claiming that he liked to bite his patients. It was Stalin's way of destroying the doctor's reputation before his arrest and murder. All the while the doctor had been keeping a file on Stalin.

In that file were facts about his heart trouble, paranoia, and his need to carry a gun in his pocket and place one under his pillow as he slept. The last sentence of the file contained Dr. Pletnov's mental diagnosis.

He determined that Stalin was a paranoid megalomaniac, meaning that he was actually mad in his need to have power. He was very suspicious and fearful of all that surrounded him. It was further broken down into a psychopathological condition characterized by fantasies of power, relevance, omnipotence, and by inflated self-esteem. The doctor's diagnosis was spot on. Stalin's mental derangement was so great that it led to the Great Purge throughout the entire country. This was a campaign of political repression and persecution in the Soviet Union, which occurred from 1934 to 1938. It was a large-scale purge of the Communist Party and governmental officials, repression of peasants and the Red Army leadership.

It resulted in widespread suspicion, beatings, forced labor, harsh imprisonment, show trials and the execution of everyone remotely suspected. During this time Stalin especially targeted the Kulaks, peasants who were lucky enough to own a farm animal, labeling them class enemies.

Kulaks were rounded up and sent to labor camps by the hundreds of thousands. Tens of thousands of men and women were interrogated, tortured, sent to hard labor or shot on site. Any commoner who objected to any of Stalin's ideas were branded a Kulak.

Under Stalin the Gulag (Soviet concentration camp) population rose from 30,000 to 2 million in just 3 years as workers suffered intolerable conditions. Millions died horrible deaths at the hands of Stalin's suspicion, paranoia and megalomania.

Stalin told to the masses that the Great Purge was revenge for the murder of Surgei Kero, the Leningrad party boss, but it is now well known that Stalin himself had Kero murdered, expanding his historic pattern of killing one rival, and then using that death to justify more killing and torture.

In reality the Great Purge happened for one reason, to kill his friends and political allies along with his enemies. Lying, twisting and spinning his ambitions to the masses through the state run media, Stalin and his mental delusions murdered anyone who knew the truth about his climb to power, the truth of his evil, or anyone who knew him well.

Suspicious to the last, his murder list included: all of the old Bolsheviks (Kemanov, Znoveov, Bukharin, Rakovsky, Krestinsky, Yagoda), anyone who knew of Lenin's last will and testament, anyone who opposed farm and industrial collectivization, ex-premier Alexei Rykov and sixteen others who belonged to the so-called "Bloc of Rightists and Trotskyites," his personal doctor of 13 years, his second wife (current wife at that time) Nadezhda Alliluyeva and all surviving relatives of both of Stalin's wives, ordering the extinction of their entire family trees.

At the peak of the purge Stalin was signing the death warrants of more than 3,000 people in one day. One by one over the course of the four years of madness Stalin brought each of the accused up on trial. He alleged a wide array of offenses before the juries in an effort to give the illusion of justice, but that was impossible as he owned and influenced everyone and everything in the court.

The results were "show trials" merely for the appearance of justice as he accused people of being everything from "enemies of the state", to plotting the "overthrow of the Soviet government", to "speaking out against Soviet collectivism."

After the "show trial" was complete and the accused found guilty (no one was ever found to be not guilty) they were taken to Lubyanka Square, the headquarters of the KGB in Meshchansky District of Moscow, and executed by being shot at point blank range in the back of the head and buried in mass graves.

Stalin's vision for his nation is defined in the following two quotes:

"Let us advance full steam ahead to become a country of metal and when we have the U.S.S.R. on a motor car and a peasant on a tractor. Then let those murched and mired capitalists try to overtake us. We'll see then whose country will be called backward and which one is advanced"

...and "One death is a tragedy... a million deaths is a statistic."

These two bone-chilling quotes have caused some historians to call him the greatest mass murderer of all time. He applied the same brutal tactics to FDR, casting his rules aside while on his way to global domination. By 1945, Roosevelt was of no use to him and actually stood to impede Stalin from his aspirations. To Stalin the war was over, the countries of Europe lay at his borders for easy domination, and he had grown tired playing FDR's way. The opportunity to murder was obvious and was timed perfectly.

Stalin knew with Roosevelt dead the agreements signed at Yalta would be voided, and he couldn't wait to unleash the beast. He wanted to settle his personal grudge with Hitler as well as grab as much real estate as he could for his expanding empire.

But before he could do this, he needed to make sure that FDR was really dead. After all, his two spies that were with Roosevelt when he collapsed at Warm Springs only saw him fall ill before they were forced to flee the scene. No one that he could really trust had actually seen FDR's corpse.

Could this be a trick? Could it be a ploy to catch him off guard so the Americans and the British could plot to overthrow him? To Stalin these were agonizing questions that lingered in his mind and they needed to be answered. He even sent someone to the casket demanding that the first lady lift the lid so they could verify that the dead man was really FDR.

After all, he didn't want Germany surrendering to the Allies, or to allow Hitler and his top brass the chance to escape. This was personal for Stalin, and Germany needed to be punished. He also couldn't wait to bulldoze the new President who had only held the position of Vice President for 2 months. He was licking his chops, but he would be disappointed.

Oscar Wilde, the Irish playwright, novelist, essayist, and poet, was quoted as saying: "There are only two tragedies in life: one is not getting what one wants, and the other is getting it." Joseph Stalin would soon understand these words in living color.

After Stalin got his long awaited prize of turning FDR into a corpse, he would come to hate Truman at first sight. Stalin's spy network in the United States had very little on Truman. Where FDR was warm and accommodating, Truman was cold, brash and stiff. Although Stalin was paranoid and suspicious of everyone in general, he took a special dislike to Harry Truman and the feeling was mutual.

Stalin wasn't very fond of Winston Churchill either, but his reason was different than his dislike of Truman. The war in Europe ended with an invasion of Germany by the Western Allies and the Soviet Union on the 8th of May, 1945. The war torn nation was completely overwhelmed by the Red Army at their door step and General Patton, along with the army of Poland, on his heels. Germany's unconditional surrender and VE Day (Victory in Europe Day) was music to the ears of the world, but now the heavy lifting of recovery by the European nations would need to begin.

In recent years, Joe Lieberman, Former United States Senator, would reflect on the situation in Europe: "It is no question that Stalin helped us defeat Nazism, but it's also true that Stalin had his eye on the post-war world and was much more focused on gaining advantage at the end of WWII which would position the Soviet Union for a greater future."

The former Senator was correct. Almost immediately, Stalin quickly mobilized the Soviet Army southward over the border into China. Truman was furious, as this was never a part of any Allied agreement.

Truman's attempt to scold Stalin remotely had little effect as Stalin had little, if any, respect for him. Truman met in Potsdam, Germany, from July 17th to August 2nd, 1945, to negotiate terms for the end of the war with Winston Churchill and Joseph Stalin.

This would come to be known as the Potsdam Conference. Truman had four goals drawn up for the conference. 1) Prevent Soviet Dominance. 2) Get an Unconditional Surrender from Japan. 3) Build democracies in Germany and Japan. 4) Avoid Future World War.

While the three men negotiated, Stalin's grand plan was beginning to unfold; much to the chagrin of the Allies, he unveiled the unthinkable. After murdering FDR, Stalin revealed another political plot to assist him in his global aspirations.

The Socialist Labour Party in England, which had been under the influence of Stalin's Communism for more than a decade, had stuffed the ballot boxes with the necessary votes and on July 26th, 1945 Winston Churchill was unexpectedly voted out of office.

From their very first meeting, Churchill had seen Stalin as a threat bigger than Hitler, but before he could neutralize Stalin by implementing his post war plan for the Allies to invade the Soviet Union and end the war on his own terms, his political legs were cut from beneath him.

After Stalin's years of carefully manipulating the Allied leaders in the same fashion that he had the leaders of the Russian government, Stalin's grand Soviet plan left the politically inexperienced Truman, and Truman alone, to establish the peace and align the countries of the world. This was like bringing the birds to the cat, and Truman was gravely outmatched – just as Stalin had planned.

With Churchill being replaced at the conference by incoming British Prime Minister, Clement Richard Attlee, the inverse power of three played out, and not in Truman's favor. Stalin had manipulated the situation and table was tilted against the wishes of the United States.

Truman ultimately failed to convince the two other leaders of his plans, failing at three of his four outlined goals. Knowing that when Stalin conquers a territory he never returns it, and fearing that the Soviet Union would make further penetration into the already volatile country of China, Truman knew that he had to act fast.

Returning to America, he immediately met with his military advisors to weigh his options. He knew that time was of the essence. The primary person that he consulted with was General Douglas MacArthur, who advised Truman to invade the Japanese islands, a military proposal that would be bloody, lengthy, and could lead to over a million US casualties.

Fearing both the time frame and the resulting carnage, Truman was forced to make a gut-wrenching decision. He ordered the dropping of the first atomic bomb on Hiroshima, Japan, a mere four days after his return from the Potsdam Conference. His goal was more than just winning the war, he was now rushing to stop Stalin and his Red Army, from overtaking the world.

With the formal Japanese surrender on September 2, 1945, today recognized as VJ Day, the Second World War came to a close – but America's problems with Stalin were just beginning. Step for step, move for move, Truman and Stalin would spend the next eight years sparring with each other in a global chess match for the world's balance of ideological power.

Although the Bolshevik revolution provided a temporary "time out" in the tensions between the Soviets and the western countries, it wouldn't last. Tensions rose to a quick boil after the end of the war and, almost as if two bullies existed on the same city block, and the huge inevitable fight was brewing.

On March 5, 1946, in a speech at Westminster College in Fulton, Missouri, the newly out of office Winston Churchill uttered the words that the world would come to know all too well for the next fifty years.

Churchill condemned the Soviet Union's policies in Europe, which would spark off the Cold War. He warned against the expansionistic policies of the Soviet Union. When he said the words "iron curtain" to describe the line between the two ideologies in Eastern Europe, the world listened. Churchill, who never liked or trusted Stalin, knew what was coming and he used this speech to ready the world.

Truman listened intently. At the time of that speech, what President Truman didn't know and was later told, was that the British Empire was greatly weakened by the fighting of World War II and could no longer provide the Greek and Turkish governments the financial aid that they needed to survive.

Churchill was gravely concerned that both countries could fall into the Soviets' hands; not only spreading their ideology but turning those countries into enemy states. 1946 through 1953 were turbulent times as the world realized that Churchill was correct in his words.

Realizing the new threat that Stalin had become to the war ravaged European nations, the United States started an initiative that was named after General George Marshall, called the Marshall Plan. The plan was to give $13 billion dollars in economic support to help rebuild the European economies, primarily Germany, Poland, and their neighbors.

While it was touted as a great humanitarian effort by the United States, that was not its true purpose. Its true design was to keep the middle of Europe from falling prey to Stalin and the Communist spread. Aid flowed freely to sixteen European nations, accompanied by the Truman Policy which helped Greece and Turkey, as well as the British Empire, financially.

The Truman Doctrine stated for the first time that U.S. policy was opposed to the expansion of Communism anywhere in the world. Both plans were designed to counter the Soviet geopolitical spread of Communism, but neither was entirely successful.

Following Stalin's blockade of West Berlin to gain control of the city, the United States and Great Britain responded with the successful Berlin Airlift of food and other provisions to the citizens of West Berlin between 1948 and 1949.

In 1948, President Truman refused to give aid to the People's Republic of China and their long fought revolutionary war. Shortly thereafter, the city of Manchuria fell to the forces led by Communist leader Mao Tse-tung, who realized that he could exert more influence on their citizens than the industrialized Western powers.

The result was the Communist takeover of the entire country. America not only lost the huge country to the spread of Communism but it also lost all of its military equipment and other provisions that it had been supplying to China.

There was no rest for Truman as Stalin was testing him yet again. In 1950, the Korean War began when North Korea, supported by the Soviet Union and Communist China, crossed the 38th parallel and invaded South Korea, which was supported by the United States.

As Kim Il-sung's North Korean Army, armed with Soviet tanks and other munitions, quickly overran South Korea, the United States came to South Korea's aid. Although Dean Gooderham Acheson, Truman's Secretary of State, thought that Korea lay outside the defensive sphere of the United States, the invasion was too blatant to be ignored.

General MacArthur, leader of the United Nations forces, drove the North Koreans back across the divide, but encountered a fierce invasion by the Chinese. The Korean War was eventually fought to a bloody draw.

At every turn Stalin was testing Truman's will and leadership ability. From the minute that he became president in 1945 until 1953, the year Stalin died and Truman left the White House, the two butted heads, countries, militaries and ideologies. Stalin and his aggressive advance of Soviet Communism were on one side, and Truman with his efforts to thwart his advances on the other.

None of this would have happened had FDR lived. President Roosevelt was an awful economic president but there was one area that he excelled beyond almost every other leader in the modern world; he was an excellent war president who was capable of both war and peace with equal skill.

Admittedly, I am not much of a Franklin Roosevelt fan, but when it came to commanding military power and negotiating savvy he was head and shoulders above the pack. Had he lived, the Cold War would not have happened and if tensions between the countries did rise, they wouldn't have lasted until 1991.

All totaled there were 87 conflicts related to the Cold War. The following list was taken from Wikipedia illustrating different Communist advances and struggles that the United States and its allies were forced to fight off. It reads like a worldwide map of war.

War in Vietnam (1945–46)

Iran crisis of 1946

Greek Civil War

Corfu Channel incident

Hukbalahap Rebellion

First Indochina War

1948 Czechoslovak coup d'état

Malayan Emergency

Berlin Blockade

Korean War

Egyptian Revolution of 1952

Uprising of 1953 in East Germany

Cuban Revolution

1953 Iranian coup d'état

Laotian Civil War

1954 Guatemalan coup d'état

First Taiwan Strait Crisis

Vietnam War

Poznań 1956 protests

Hungarian Revolution of 1956

Suez Crisis

14 July Revolution

Second Taiwan Strait Crisis

1959 Tibetan uprising

1960 U-2 incident

Congo Crisis

Angolan War of Independence

Bay of Pigs Invasion

Berlin Crisis of 1961

Nicaraguan Revolution

Cuban Missile Crisis

Sino-Indian War

Guinea-Bissau War of Independence

1964 Brazilian coup d'état

Rhodesian Bush War

Mozambican War of Independence

Dominican Civil War

US occupation of the Dominican Republic (1965–66)

Indo-Pakistani War of 1965

30 September Movement

Indonesian killings of 1965–66

South African Border War

Namibian War of Independence

Greek military junta of 1967–74

Six-Day War

War of Attrition

Communist Insurgency War

Sino-Soviet border conflict

1969 Libyan coup d'état

Black September in Jordan

Cambodian Civil War

First Quarter Storm

Bangladesh Liberation War

Indo-Pakistani War of 1971

1973 Chilean coup d'état

Yom Kippur War

Carnation Revolution

Ethiopian Civil War

Cambodian–Vietnamese War

Lebanese Civil War

Angolan Civil War

Indonesian invasion of East Timor

Operation Entebbe

1976 Argentine coup d'état

Shaba I

Mozambican Civil War

Ethio-Somali War

Shaba II

Korean Air Lines Flight 902

Iranian Revolution

Sino-Vietnamese War

Salvadoran Civil War

Soviet war in Afghanistan

1982 Ethiopian–Somali Border War

Korean Air Lines Flight 007

Invasion of Grenada

People Power Revolution

1986 United States bombing of Libya

8888 Uprising

United States invasion of Panama

Revolutions of 1989

Tiananmen Square protests of 1989

Velvet Revolution

Mongolian Revolution of 1990

Romanian Revolution

Gulf War

1991 Soviet coup d'état attempt

When President Roosevelt's head slumped to one side and he drew his last breath, he had no idea that he had Joseph Stalin to thank for it. He had no idea that Stalin was a megalomaniac and a master of fulfilling his desires, carving his political path in life by assassinating anyone and everyone in his way.

He had no idea about the number of Soviet spies that existed in his White House, or that they had infiltrated every governmental department at high levels. He had no idea that his closest political confidante, Harry Hopkins, as well as the artist that was sitting before him when he closed his eyes for the last time, Elizabeth Shoumatoff, were leaking information directly back to Stalin himself.

There was no way for the President to know that he was systematically being poisoned by the White House cook because the food was so horrible on a regular basis that he couldn't detect it. What he did know was that he had been fighting a see-saw battle between life and death from a mysterious illness for over two years and that the most competent physicians in the country were baffled as to its cause.

He also knew that his body as well as his mind was being adversely effected before, during, and after the Yalta Conference, but his arrogance and his pride were so great that he wouldn't relinquish his command for the good of the country or the world.

Privileged, smug, pompous, and philandering to the last, he was so involved with his self-importance and his sexual promiscuity that he failed to ask himself the one question that would have saved his life: How in God's name could food in the White House consistently be that bad without it being intentional? I have no doubt that some people will continue to believe that the mole over the president's eyebrow indicated that he died as a result of a melanoma.

This was the hypothesis in the 2011 book, *FDR's Deadly Secret*. To those people I pose the following question: If indeed the brown blob over the president's eyebrow was cancerous, how and why did FDR's health see-saw so drastically? He was near death one day and then rebounding to the brink of vibrancy the day after. He did this for two years. To my knowledge, an untreated melanoma would not have behaved in such a capacity.

If he did have a cancerous melanoma he would have just faded away slowly, growing weaker and weaker until he finally expired, but that wasn't at all what history revealed. In fact, history tells us of a rollercoaster ride of health that became President Roosevelt's life from the Conference in Tehran to the Conference in Yalta.

This is not possible for a terminally ill cancer patient. From my findings on this matter, which were based on exhaustive research, and according to each of his many doctors, FDR's death was not the result of the advance of his polio either.

His symptoms simply didn't align with them. With both cancer and polio ruled out as a cause of death, the glaring reality is that each and every symptom that the president was suffering from, and eventually succumbed to, perfectly aligned with lead poisoning.

This is the only thing that could account for his constant rebounds of health and the missed diagnoses of his many doctors. So with that said, I will end this book in the same way that I ended *Who Murdered Elvis?*, by reminding everyone that I didn't write this book for myself, I wrote it for all of you.

The truth might hurt, but it should never be hidden, and the truth must bust through the decades of lies that we have been fed and that we continue to feed the next generation through the elongated agenda of academia.

Fortunately, there are a few of us who desire real answers and who refuse to simply roll over on command. Eleanor Roosevelt was one of those people. Nearly a decade after FDR's death, she ordered a private investigation into the truth.

With the help of a private investigator she dug into FDR's medical care as well as his odd death. The results were never released. I must wonder, did she decide to take the facts of the investigation to her grave on her own initiative, or was she gagged by those in power within our own government?

Since we will never know, that is a question that you must answer for yourself. There are times when we want there to be more to a story that there really is because we refuse to believe that obvious truth, and then there are times that there truly is more to a story. You have no idea how much I wish the words *conspiracy theory* were removed from our vernacular because it is so irresponsible to label every conspiracy as false and every theorist as a nutcase. After all, the legal term of Conspiracy exists for a reason.

Contrary to popular opinion I am not a conspiracy theorist, I am a reality theorist. I believe that President Roosevelt died from a cerebral hemorrhage as history suggests, but the makings of that cause of death were not natural. There is no doubt that remains in my mind who murdered him or how it was done.

If you agree with me or disagree with me that is a decision that you will have to make for yourself, but one thing is certain, now that you have read this book, you share the burden of this knowledge. What you do with this knowledge is entirely up to you. Make your decision wisely while remembering this quote from Joseph Stalin: *"Death solves all problems. No man, no problems."*

This volume and the volumes that follow solve histories mysteries and make great conversation pieces. For all of your gift giving needs visit the book series website.
www.whomurderedbooks.com

CPSIA information can be obtained
at www.ICGtesting.com
Printed in the USA
FSHW020821070120
65643FS